THE PROJECT
COOL GUIDE
TO HTML

THE PROJECT COOL GUIDE

TO HTML

TERESA A. MARTIN *and* GLENN DAVIS

John Wiley & Sons, Inc.
New York • Chichester • Brisbane • Toronto • Singapore • Weinheim

Publisher: Katherine Schowalter
Editor: Tim Ryan
Assistant Editor: Pam Sobotka
Assistant Managing Editor: Carl Germann
Text Design & Composition: North Market Street Graphics, Selena R. Chronister

This text is printed on acid-free paper.

This publication is designed to provide accurate and authoritative information in regard to the subject matter covered. It is sold with the understanding that the publisher is not engaged in rendering legal, accounting, or other professional service. If legal advice or other expert assistance is required, the services of a competent professional person should be sought.

Library of Congress Cataloging-in-Publication Data:
Martin, Teresa A. 1961–
    The project cool guide to HTML / Glenn Davis and Teresa Martin.
       p.   cm.
    Includes bibliographical references.
    ISBN 0-471-17371-1 (pbk. : alk. paper)
    1. HTML (Document markup language) I. Davis, Glenn, 1961– .
II. Title.
QA76.76.H94M275 1997
005.7'2—dc20
                            96-35308
                              CIP

Printed in the United States of America
10 9 8 7 6 5 4 3 2 1

Once, when televisions came in black-and-white and long distance phone calls were just for special occasions, a six-year-old persisted in showing her mother endless drafts of a book crafted in vivid green felt-tip pen. So this book (with nary a trace of green marker!) is for my mother— because I promised.

—TERESA A. MARTIN

To my children: Nicole, Logan, and Cassie. They'll get to see the Web evolve into something we are only just beginning to see a glimmer of. And to one other, who shall remain nameless.

—GLENN DAVIS

CONTENTS

CONTENTS

CONTENTS

INTRODUCTION: PUBLISHING'S NEW ERA

Back in the early 1980s, there was a sudden boom in publishing. Affordable personal computers complete with fonts and simple layout tools and small, clean laser printers landed on our desktops, and people who couldn't be publishers before suddenly had power to create, print, and distribute. Desktop publishing was here.

It was an interesting era for publishing. It was an exciting era for publishing. New voices appeared as the barriers to entry fell. But it was also a visually ugly era.

You see, although everyone *could* publish, not everyone could publish *well*. And so we ended up with corporate memos that looked like ransom notes with 22 different variations of type. The person writing the memo suddenly had the power to control the look and feel—and used this power as many times as possible in each document. Newsletters, once typed on a typewriter, could have columns and clip art—and did and did and did. New magazines sprouted, created by people who were just exploring type, design, and layout, learning as they went. Many publications out there just weren't good examples of publishing. But people learned, publications survived, and the concept of desktop publishing has become so integrated into our way of thinking that we don't even separate it out as a special type of publishing technology anymore.

Today, we have an entity called the World Wide Web. Like desktop publishing, it helps us create and distribute information. It's a publishing medium. And, once again, it has dropped the barrier to entry by providing new tools and technologies for publishing. Nearly anyone can do it. However, not everyone is doing it well. Funny how history repeats itself.

We've been building and watching the Web since 1993, and we've seen it evolve from basic text and links into a full-fledged medium. It's a wonderfully dynamic publishing environment, and, with a little knowledge, your Web site will be one of the good examples on the Web. The book you hold in your hand is our effort to help you survive the glut of uninspiring publishing on the Web and create your own site that stands out from the pack.

You see, we're not going to just help you learn HTML. There's so much more to building a Web site than entering HTML code. We're going to help you with the whys as well as the hows. Why would I want to use a table instead of preformatted text? When do I use a frame? Why use an imagemap? Don't worry if those terms sound unfamiliar to you. By the time we're done, you'll not only know what they are and how to use them, but you'll know when to use them and why. That's important. It can make the difference between a Web site and a *cool* Web site.

Cool. Now there's an interesting term. On the one hand, it can be pretty subjective, but everyone seems to know what it is when they see it. When we say *cool,* we have some definite things in mind. *Cool* is about quality; about something done well; about something useful; about something that shows information in a new way; about something that reaches out, grabs your attention, and makes it worth your while to stop by.

A cool Web site doesn't need to be one that whistles, spins, and has flashy, fancy animation. It does need to have good writing and a design that is both visually appealing and appropriate for the information. Its content needs to be useful, organized, and accurate. The graphics must be clean and original. The execution of the site must be done well, with the best technology and the best applications for the job. A cool site is interactive—it pulls in the reader and doesn't just sit there on the screen, blinking mindlessly. It integrates different varieties of information; its parts have a certain synergy with each other. The whole site holds together and invites the reader to stop and stay for a while. You want to show a cool site to your friends. And you want to visit it again and again. Now that's cool.

In this book, we'll give you some ideas for how to make a cool Web site. And we'll show you some sites that are done well and introduce you to the people and thoughts behind them.

We'll also give you an interactive place to test your new skills.

THIS BOOK COMES WITH ITS OWN WEB SITE

This book comes with its own Web site. Because the best way to learn is by doing, we've built a special section on the Web where you can practice your HTML and immediately see the results.

Throughout this book we've included Try This sections. The Try This sections look like this:

 TRY THIS: Go to the Try This Web site and type this sentence.

These sections are examples that you can create in the Try It page of the Project Cool's Guide to HMTL Web site. In some cases, we've also placed supporting material, such as images, on the Web site so that you can practice using an image without having to create one from scratch.

To use the site, all you need is a computer with a connection to the Internet and a Web browser. You don't need any special software. You don't need any special type of computer—any Macintosh, PC, or UNIX computer can access the site. You don't have to load anything onto your hard drive. Heck, you don't even need your own computer. Most public libraries and other community centers now offer access to the Internet. With this book and a connected computer, you can learn how to build a Web page.

Figure I.1 shows what the Web site looks like.

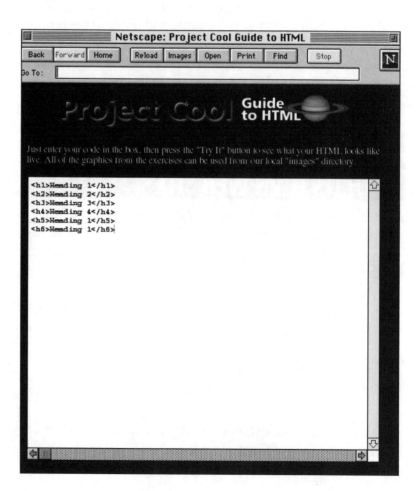

Figure I.1
The Try It section of this book's Web site.

You'll see that it has a large area for typing text and a Try It button. When you click on the Try It button, the HTML tags and text that you've typed appear as they would in a Web browser. You can quickly get a feel for the tags and the results they produce. You can edit them and see how they change. You can get instant gratification and reinforce what you've read.

GETTING TO THE WEB SITE

Getting to the Web site is easy. To get there:

1. Start your Web browser. (If you don't know how to use a Web browser, read Chapter 1, which introduces you to the Web and how to browse it.)

2. Enter this URL in the browser bar and then press RETURN: http://www.projectcool.com/guide/html

3. The Try It page should appear in your browser window.

TIP: *Once you've been to the Try It page, save it as a bookmark (see Chapter 1). Then, you can just select it from the bookmark list to get there quickly and easily.*

USING THE WEB SITE

Using the Web site is easy, too. To use the Web site:

1. Click into the text window.

2. Type the HTML tags and text that you want to try using.

3. Click on TRY IT. The tags and text now appear as a Web page.

That's all there is to it! So good luck . . . and welcome to the Web.

ACKNOWLEDGMENTS

We'd like to thank all the people who have helped us along this book-project route, including Jim Sterne, who helped launch the process; Tim and Pam, our editors at Wiley; everyone who has ever participated in a Project Cool class or workshop; NASA for its image inspiration; and the thousands of designers, developers, creators, and dreamers who are building this medium called the Web.

THE PROJECT
COOL GUIDE
TO HTML

GETTING STARTED ON THE WEB

Imagine a book with an infinite number of pages. Any page can reference any other page, and a reader can easily jump from one page to the other and back again. New pages are added all the time, by different people in different locations. Now take that book and spread its pages around the globe. And there you have the World Wide Web.

The World Wide Web (WWW or the Web, for short) is revolutionizing the way we work with information. Many people (including those of us at Project Cool) think that the Web is a new medium, one that we're just learning to use.

In technical terms, the Web is an easy-to-use graphical user interface to the *Internet,* the international "network of networks" of computers. The original Internet infrastructure was created more than 25 years ago as part of a U.S. Department of Defense project. The notion of a network of networks came out of the need to create a computer communication system capable of withstanding nuclear attack and other Cold War fears. The idea was that if one part of the network went out, information flow could quickly be rerouted. Additionally, information could "live" on many different computers, so that emergency backup was practically built in.

World Wide Web (WWW)—A graphical interface to the Internet. Often simply called "the Web."

Internet—A global network of computers sharing information using certain agreed-upon standards.

Because using the Internet required a certainly level of technical know-how and special telecommunication connections, most people who used the Internet were in government, research, or academia. Until the Web came along, that is.

The Web changed everything. Suddenly, navigating the Internet was as simple as pointing and clicking. You didn't have to type in UNIX commands. Using a structure called *HTML,* information could be displayed in type at different sizes with color and graphics. And, most importantly, information could be linked to other information. Figure 1.1 shows a sample Web page.

The concept of *hypertext* is central to the Web. Hypertext is the idea of linking together content across many different locations. When you click on a hypertext link, you automatically see the related information. It's a little like the way the human brain works—you know, you're thinking about high school and you remember Mr. King, the math teacher, which makes you remember the theorem "*a=b, b=c,* therefore *a=c,*" which makes you think of the philosopher/

Hypertext Markup Language (HTML)— The codes used to create a page of text and graphics that can be viewed using the World Wide Web.

hypertext—Text that links to other information.

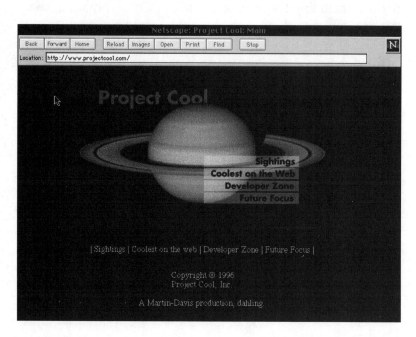

Figure 1.1
A Web page. Notice how text and graphics can be combined to make navigation easier than a line of UNIX code.

mathematician Descartes because his minibiography was in your math book, and you remember that Descartes said, "I think, therefore I am," which makes you think about the meaning of life, and so on. On the Web, using the HTML structure, you can build real links between a picture of Mr. King to a page of mathematical theorems to a set of quotes of philosophers to a page that ponders the meaning of life. If someone is interested, that person just clicks on the links to call up the related information. Figure 1.2 shows how hypertext connects thoughts.

GETTING ON THE WEB

To use the Web today, you need three things:

▶ A computer

▶ A Web *browser*

▶ A connection to the Internet that supports the Web

The computer can be any type of recent vintage machine. Macintoshes, Windows machines, and UNIX boxes all sup-

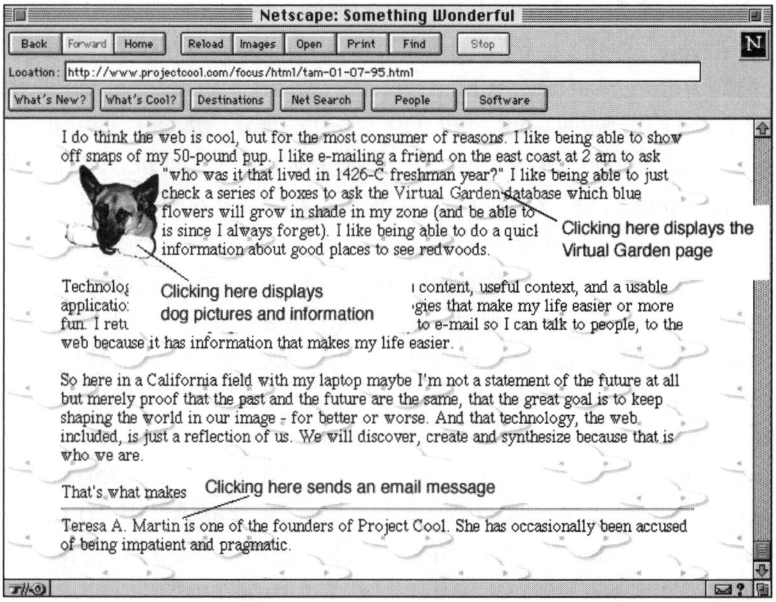

browser—A computer program that lets you see WWW pages on your computer screen.

Figure 1.2
Information links on the Web.

port the Web. Of course, the faster the machine and the more memory it has, the more satisfied you'll be with your Web experience.

The Web browser is the tool you use to move around the Web. The browser displays text, graphics, and links on your computer screen and interprets the HTML commands. The two most common browsers are Netscape's Navigator and Microsoft's Internet Explorer. A third common browser, especially among UNIX users, is NCSA's Mosaic. (NCSA stands for the National Center for Supercomputing Applications; NCSA is part of the University of Illinois at Urbana/Champaign. This is where Marc Andreesen, cofounder of Netscape Communications Corporation, worked as a student and was part of the team that created Mosaic, the original Web browser.) Figure 1.3 shows the two most common browsers. On the top is Netscape Navigator; on the bottom is Microsoft's Internet Explorer. They both fill the same role, but their look and feel varies slightly.

TIP: *The browser market is very competitive. Both Netscape and Microsoft are bringing out new versions of their respective browsers every few months. Each new version adds new features, but the basic function—displaying a Web page—remains the same.*

However, Web site development keeps changing to take advantage of the features the newest browsers offer. To see Web sites in the best light, you'll probably want to update your browser software every six months or so until the market stabilizes. If you don't update, you'll still be able to use the Web, but you may not see every page at its best.

The connection to the Internet can come from many different places. If you are dialing in from a modem at home, you'll want something called Point-to-Point Protocol (PPP) or Serial Link Internet Protocol (SLIP). PPP and SLIP let you use the Web to navigate the Internet. You can get these connections from a local Internet Service Provider (an ISP); through one of the commercial online services such as AOL, CompuServe, or Prodigy; or through a telecommunications company such as AT&T or MCI. These companies will also

Point-to-Point Protocol (PPP)— A type of telecommunication connection that lets you use the Web via a modem.

Serial Link Internet Protocol (SLIP)—A type of telecommunication connection that lets you use the Web via a modem.

Internet Service Provider (ISP)— The company that provides you with a connection to the Internet.

supply you with the connection software you need to dial into their services.

Shop around for the best local connection in your area. Prices are falling as more and more people offer these ser-

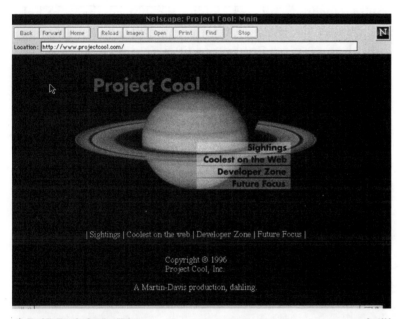

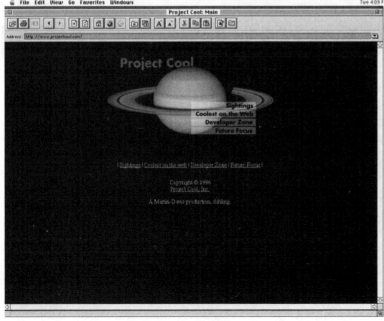

Figure 1.3
Netscape Navigator and Microsoft's Internet Explorer.

vices. You can probably find a connection that gives you an e-mail account, unlimited Web connection time, and a limited amount of space for storing your own Web pages for $19.95 or less per month. Make sure you feel comfortable with your ISP and its customer support. Setting up the connection is a little different with each provider, and unless you're a technical wizard, you'll probably call them for help at least once. Don't let this scare you off the Web—it's not difficult to set up; it just takes a little time up front to do it.

If you are accessing the Web through a modem, get the fastest modem you can. Many people have 14.4-kilobaud modems (the higher the number, the faster information will move over it); this is the lowest common denominator for using the Web. A 28.8 modem is better. And if you have money to burn, you might want to find an ISP that supports Integrated Services Digital Network (ISDN) connections and add ISDN service to your home or business. If you are connecting from an office, your company might have a T1 or a T3 telecommunication line, which is very fast. But most people connect to the Web through a modem, either at 14.4 or 28.8.

BROWSING BASICS

There's some Web lingo that you'll hear over and over again. It might sound a little overwhelming at first, but most of the acronyms make sense, and within days you'll find them popping right out of your mouth.

The URL

The Uniform Resource Locator, or URL, describes where to find something on the Web. It is written like this:

```
http://www.projectcool.com
```

This is the address you type into your Web browser to see a specific page. (A *page* is a specific file on the Web.)

Integrated Services Digital Network (ISDN)— A type of telecommunications service that is available from your local telephone company. To connect to the Web via ISDN, you need both the service and a special ISDN modem.

Uniform Resource Locator (URL)— The full, exact name of a file on the Web.

page—A single file on the Web.

The URL has three parts.

▶ The *http://* tells the browser that it will be going to a place that uses hypertext transfer protocol—that is, it will be looking at a Web page.

▶ The *www.projectcool* part is the name of the Web site. (A Web site is a collection of related pages.) In this example, the site is called "projectcool."

▶ The .com portion describes the type of site. You might see .com for commercial; .edu for education; .net for Internet provider; .org for nonprofit organization; .gov for government; or .nz, .uk, .jp, .au, .nl, or other country abbreviation for a particular country.

Web site—A collection of related pages, linked together, that work as a single entity.

Browser Controls

You can control some of the ways you see the Web by setting different default values in your browser. You might want to set a font style and size, background and text colors, or other look and feel controls. There's nothing wrong with continuing to use the default values, however.

TIP: *This is important to remember later on, when you are building your own Web page or Web site. Not everyone is going to see your page the same way you do; different people set different defaults for their browsers. Some leave the defaults, while others override them.*

Web-Page Parts

A typical Web page will have several parts, as illustrated in Figure 1.4.

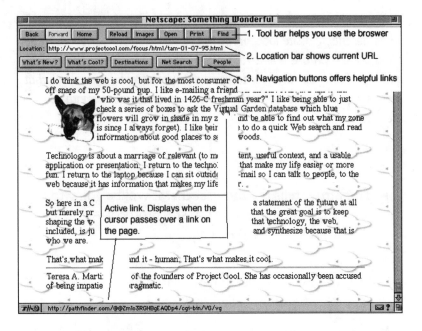

Figure 1.4
Parts of a browser. In this example, the Netscape Navigator browser is shown, but all browsers are similiar.

▶ Your current URL—the one that describes the page you are looking at—appears in a bar at either the top or the bottom of the browser window. Exactly where it appears depends on which browser you are using.

▶ The title of the page will appear in the browser window's title bar.

▶ In the main window will be some text. There will probably be some graphics or images too. Sometimes the graphics will appear as little boxes with a circle, square, and triangle. This means that for some reason—a break in the transmission, a problem with the graphic file—your browser can't display that particular graphic just now. You can click on the Reload button in your browser to attempt to get the graphics to load onto your screen.

▶ There might be sound or animation. Sound and animation are often noted by an icon.

▶ At various places in the page will be links. Links are usually visually identified by having the linked text underlined or in a different color, or having a colored box around the linked graphic. As you move your cursor around the page, you'll notice that sometimes a URL other than your current one appears in the status. That's because every time you pass the cursor over a link, the URL of the link appears. You can see where you are going before you click to actually go there.

USING YOUR BROWSER

Each variety of Web browser looks a little different, but they all share some basic functions. This section outlines those basic functions.

Connecting to the Net

Before you start your browser software, it is a good idea to establish a connection to the Internet or your company's intranet. If you're accessing the Web from a modem, this means dialing your modem and connecting via SLIP or PPP. If you are within a company setting connected to a network, you may have access all the time and don't need to do anything special.

Default Pages

When you launch your browser, it will automatically go to a default home page. You can set the default home page to be any Web page you want. Typically, the vendors of the browser software set the default to be their own home page. In an intranet, the home page is typically the internal Web's home page. You can change this setting at any time.

Selecting a Site

You tell your browser to display a particular Web page by typing that page's URL into the browser's selection bar. In most browsers, this bar is near the top of the page. On some browsers, such as Netscape Navigator, you can omit the "http://" part of the URL.

To select a site:

1. Type the URL in the selection bar.
2. Press RETURN.
3. The browser displays the specified page.

Using RELOAD

One of the buttons in the browser command bar is labeled
RELOAD. If the page you asked for doesn't come in fully or
comes in with broken graphics or another problem, try clicking on RELOAD. This tells the browser to ask for the current
page again.

Using BACK

Another button in the browser's command bar is labeled
BACK. You'll quickly become familiar with this button.
Each time you click on BACK, you go back one page. Click
on BACK three times and you go back to the page you had
on your screen three pages ago. The BACK button, along
with its mate FORWARD, make it easy to move among a
set of Web pages.

Using GO

GO is also in the browser's command bar. This button keeps
a list of the most recent pages you have displayed on your
screen. Click and hold down GO and you'll see a pulldown
or pop-up menu of those pages. You can jump directly to
any of them by selecting the one you want.

Using BOOKMARK

Sometimes you come across a page that you know you'll
want to visit again and again. You can easily put a bookmark
on this page for quick reference. The name of the book-

marked page will be added to the Bookmark pulldown or pop-up menu that appears when you click on BOOKMARK in the command bar. You can jump directly to any one of these pages by selecting the name from the menu.

Using STOP

Sometimes a page tries and tries and tries to load and you just run out of patience. You can stop the loading process by clicking on STOP in the browser command bar.

Web Errors

The Web isn't perfect. It is still young, and it is growing so fast that sometimes you won't be able to connect to the site you want for a variety of reasons. Maybe the server is busy. Or maybe there is a glitch in one piece of the computer network. The URL name might be old or inaccurate, or something might be wrong with the site.

When you can't connect, you'll receive an error message on your screen. The most common message is a vague NOT FOUND or SERVER CAN'T CONNECT. When you see an error message, first check the URL to make sure you've entered it correctly. Then, try the site again. Often, you'll get through on the second or even the third try.

If you get repeated CAN'T CONNECT messages from different URLs, the problem may lie in your ISP. Sometimes parts of your service provider's system go down, preventing you from browsing the Web.

The most common reasons you can't connect are:

▶ *You've entered an incorrect URL—a very easy thing to do.* It's amazing how computers only do exactly what we tell them and not what we really mean for them to do. If you leave out a slash or a dot, you'll get an error, so double check your typing carefully.

▶ *Your request is getting lost someplace on the Net.* The Internet is very heavily used. Sometimes you can't get to a site because some part of the path that the data wants to move along is blocked, slowed down, or temporarily out of order. That's why it is always smart to try loading a site a second time after you receive an error message. The Internet will route the data along different paths each time, and you may well receive the requested site on the second try.

▶ *The site has moved or is no longer available.* If you are going to a site from a link elsewhere on the Web, the referring page might be pointing you to a URL that no longer exists. In cyberspace, like outer space, you find a lot of odd bits of debris floating around—there are phantom sites, abandoned sites, and traces of servers that once were. Until there is some sort of garbage collection service, dead links are just part of the landscape.

▶ *Your ISP is having problems.* Although ISPs are generally improving, no computer system is immune to crashes, overloads, or other problems. If you can't access any sites, your connection to the Web may contain the problem. Call your ISP's customer support line and report the problem.

And Browse!

Once you get on the Web, spend some time just browsing around, following links that interest you, and exploring what is out there. The best way to understand how the Web works it to use it.

If you don't know where to start, try some of the lists of links. For example, Project Cool—http://www.projectcool. com—picks a Daily Cool Sighting and keeps an archive of past picks. It also has a Coolest on the Web section that shows some good examples of Web-site design.

BUILDING A WEB PRESENCE

Once you get on the Web and spend some time looking around, you'll probably want to create your own space on the Web. Your space can be as simple as a single page or a complex as an entire Web site. Your space can represent you, your hobbies, or your business. People are using the Web to communicate with far-flung family and friends, advertise their goods and services, deliver information, and sell products. What you do with your Web space is limited mostly by your imagination and the time and effort you put into building it.

The basic Web-site building process has three steps:

1. Create your pages on your own computer.

2. Test the pages on your own computer, viewing them with your Web browser.

3. Transfer the files from your computer to your ISP's computer, where other people go to access them.

Tools

To build a Web page, you'll need only a few simple tools:

▶ A text editor that can save text as an ASCII file.

▶ A graphics program than can save files in standard format (see Chapter 2). Adobe's Photoshop is one of the most widely used programs. Adobe is less expensive and more basic. Photo Deluxe might also be an option if you are not a heavy user of graphic programs.

▶ A Web browser. You'll use the OPEN FILE function to see an HTML file on your local hard drive.

▶ A program for transferring files from your computer to the place they'll be stored and accessed by others. Most

text editor—A simple program for writing and editing text that saves files in ASCII text format. Ideal for creating HTML pages.

ASCII—American Standard Code for Information Interchange. A standard for representing letters, numbers, punctuation, and control codes in a computer file.

GETTING STARTED ON THE WEB

13

people with a Macintosh use a program called Fetch. Most people with a PC use a program called WSftp. Typically, your ISP will give you the appropriate program and directions for using it to transfer data to their computers.

Domain Names

If you are using your Web site for business, you might want to register a domain name of your own. Every computer on the Web is identified by an IP number. This is a group of four different numbers, each separated by a period. The numbers look something like this: 174.123.111.234. The domain name matches an easy-to-remember word with the IP number, so that users can just point their browsers to www.joesbar.com rather than having to remember a not-very-memorable number. A domain name costs $50 to register and a yearly fee to keep. Domain names are registered and tracked by a group called the InterNIC, which started out as a volunteer organization but is now a for-profit company. If you move your Web site to another computer, you can change the number that matches it. Your visitors still find you by typing www.joesbar.com, but the domain name service sends them to the correct computer.

Most often, you will get your domain name through your Internet provider. Not all Internet providers allow you to have your own domain name; if this is important to you, make sure you ask about it when selecting a provider.

If you are creating a personal page, you may just want to use the domain name of your Internet provider. You'll be storing your Web page on one of their computers. The address of your page will be their domain name, followed by the subdirectory in which your files are stored. For example: www.projectcool.com/homepages/martin. If you are doing this, your provider will tell you what your URL is.

domain name— The textual name of an Internet address. Internet addresses are really a series of numbers; the domain name was introduced as an in-between, more human-friendly way to navigate the Internet.

IP address, IP number— The numeric Internet address.

domain name service (DNS)— A service provided by a program on a host computer that converts a textual domain name into the IP address that Internet software uses to find a computer on the Internet.

PLANNING YOUR WEB SITE

Before you go off and build your Web page or Web site, sit down with pencil and paper and sketch out what you want to do. What components will be part of the site? Who is your audience? What do you want people who are reading your site to do?

Remember, you don't build Web sites in a vacuum. You build them for someone. That someone might be yourself, your friends, or your prospective customers. The needs of your readers will help determine what you do with your site. For example, if you are creating a site for people who will be using it at their jobs, and they are likely to have T1 or other fast telecommunication connections, you might use more graphics than you would if most of your visitors will be connecting to the Web through a 14.4 modem.

Bandwidth is one of the biggest factors in designing a Web site. Bandwidth describes the size of "pipe" through which your reader is connecting to the Web. A 14.4 modem is a very small pipe that can be overwhelmed by a high bandwidth design—your readers will end up waiting and waiting for your pages to load. Items like large graphics, video, and animations fill up bandwidth very quickly. There are a number of things you can do to give the appearance of high bandwidth, while in reality using only a very low bandwidth. We'll talk about some of those things in Chapter 9.

Plug-ins are one way of adding additional types of information to your Web page or Web site. These miniprograms work within the browser and let you incorporate different kinds of data, such as video, audio, and animation, seamlessly within your HTML pages. In Chapter 11, we'll talk about some of the more common plug-ins and why you might want to consider using them.

Once you start building Web pages, you'll quickly find more and more things you want to do on the Web. Maybe

bandwidth—Used to describe the size of the "pipeline" through which data moves between computers. High bandwidth means lots of data can flow at one time. Low bandwidth means less data can flow at one time.

plug-ins—Small programs that work with your browser to let you see other types of data besides HTML files.

it's as basic as showing your geographically dispersed family the latest set of baby pictures. Or perhaps it's working on your company's intranet. Maybe you're showing a gallery of your artwork to potential buyers. The possibilities are endless.

It might not feel completely intuitive at first, but the more you browse and see different sites and experiment with your own, the more natural the Web medium will feel . . . and before you know it, you'll be well on your way to calling yourself a Web builder.

2

UNDERSTANDING HTML

Hypertext markup language (HTML) is the basic building block of the World Wide Web page. It is a streaming text language that uses tags to format text, create hyperlinks, and insert graphic images.

Hypertext is the idea of linking together content across many different locations. The strength of the Web lies in its ability to display seamless pages. The very name *browser* also comes from this idea—the browser lets you look at content from different locations around the world.

Your Web site will be made up of a number of HTML files. Each HTML file contains tags that tell browsers how to display your information.

HOW DOES HTML WORK?

The pages you build for the Web contain HTML tags. Tags define basic page appearances such as paragraphs, lists, and tables. They also define interactivity, such as linking to another page or letting people send you e-mail.

You store your files on a server. People read your pages with a browser, such as Netscape Navigator or Microsoft Internet Explorer. When a Web browser requests the file, the server sends across one long unbroken string of ASCII text.

tags—The control codes for building an HTML document.

hyperlinks—Text or images that perform a specific action. When the reader clicks on the hyperlinked text or graphics, the appropriate action happens.

server—A computer that responds to requests for information, "serving" up pages or data.

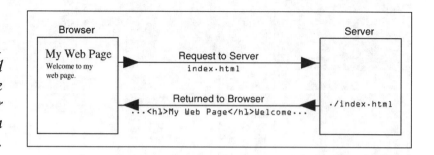

The browser turns the long string into a viewable page. Any formatting, extra spaces, or unrecognizable characters that you put into your HTML file will be completely ignored by the browser. It turns anything it doesn't understand into a single space (see Figure 2.1).

When you create an HTML page, don't try to adjust the way your final page will look by adding extra spaces in the HTML file. The browser will just ignore them. You can, however, add extra space to make the ASCII HTML source file easier to read.

HTML is the standard for creating Web pages. It is not a total solution, however. It offers limited graphical control; if you come from the type or design world, HTML limitations will become quickly apparent. Still, it does its main task of providing basic formatting and linking content very well.

HTML STANDARDS

A core set of HTML tags are considered standard and are supported by all browsers, while others are supported only by certain browsers. Netscape has been the most aggressive in introducing new HTML tags. For example, Netscape was the first to support the use of a feature called frames. In early 1996, you needed a Netscape browser in order to see frames. Now, both Mosaic and Microsoft's Internet Explorer browsers support frames as well.

When you are using nonstandard tags, it is important to remember that your HTML files may display differently on

frames—A way of breaking up a browser's display window into sub-windows.

different browsers. However, don't design for the lowest common denominator. If you do that, you'll end up with very basic, very common pages. Instead, design for your core audience.

Most of the HTML we'll talk about in this book is now supported by the major browsers. In Appendix C, we also talk about some specific Netscape and Microsoft tags that you might want to consider using if most of your readers are using one of those browsers.

HTML TOOLS

To create an HTML file, all you need is a simple text editor that can save a file as ASCII text. BBEdit Lite is a popular text editor for the Macintosh. Notepad is a popular choice for Windows machines. Some people also use word processors such as Microsoft Word or Word Perfect.

There are also a number of HTML editors. Adobe PageMill, Netscape Navigator Gold, and SoftQuad HotMetal are among the most popular commercial packages. These editors support the basic HTML tags and let you see the page as it will appear in a browser. Instead of typing tags, you can select commands from pulldown menus and click and drag items. The drawback to these editors is that they support only a subset of available tags.

An HTML editor is a good choice for you if most of your pages use tags that these editors support. Most HTML editors offer an ASCII text-editing option. Some people use an HTML editor to do most of the page, then type the actual ASCII text for the tags that the editor doesn't support.

TIP: *Even if you are using an editor, it is still important to understand how the HTML is working. It makes fixing problems easier and maximizes the effectiveness of your site.*

If your pages are going to contain graphics, you'll also need a tool that creates images and saves them as GIF or

JPEG files. GIF and JPEG are standard graphic formats. Most images on the Web are stored in one or the other of these. Adobe Photoshop is, in our opinion, the best all-around graphics tool for creating images for the Web. In Chapter 9, we'll be covering some Photoshop techniques for creating Web graphics.

HTML STRUCTURE

It is very important to create your HTML files in an orderly manner. A clear structure for your HTML documents makes them easy to read, easy to follow, and easy to modify. If you disappeared tomorrow and other people had to come in and work on your HTML files, could they figure out what you've been doing, or would they be looking at a big messy glob of tags and text? It's easy to end up with spaghetti code. That's why one of the first steps in learning how to create Web pages is to learn some simple structural guidelines.

There is no single right style or structure. What is important is that you be consistent across all files. The specific guidelines in this section are things we've found work well.

Naming Your Files

All HTML documents should have a filename extension of .html or .htm. The following are good HTML filenames:

▶ basics.html

▶ catshome.htm

▶ playerlist.html

The browser looks at the filename extension and knows to interpret the file as HTML tags rather than straight ASCII text.

Generally, if you are creating files on a Macintosh, you'll use .html as your extension. If you are creating files on a

Windows machine, you'll use .htm because a DOS PC file extension can only be three characters long.

Organizing Your Files

It may sound obvious, but maintaining a consistent and logical directory structure is the first place to bring order to your HTML files. A good directory structure makes it easier to transfer files to and from your site, and it simplifies site maintenance. Here are *two simple* rules that really help to organize your files.

1. *Use subdirectories that mimic the structure of your site.* For example, if your Web site is about animals, you might have a subdirectory for each animal: cats, dogs, horses.

2. *Separate different file types within the subdirectories.* For example, put all the images for the cats section together within the cats subdirectory.

This type of structure makes it easier to keep track of your site as it grows. Figure 2.2 shows an example of how a site about dogs and dog training might be structured. If you put a structure in place like this at the beginning, then you won't be faced with a cataloging mess later.

Tag Parts

The basic HTML tag has four parts:

► An opening delimiter, the less-than (<) symbol.

► The tag name.

► One or more switches that set variables for the tag.

► A closing delimiter, the greater-than (>) symbol.

A typical HTML tag might look something like this. This is the paragraph tag with the align switch set to center the text:

```
<p align=center>
```

delimiter—A character or command that indicates the boundaries of a section.

switches—Controls found within HTML tags that set different characteristics for that tag.

variables—Values that change.

UNDERSTANDING HTML

21

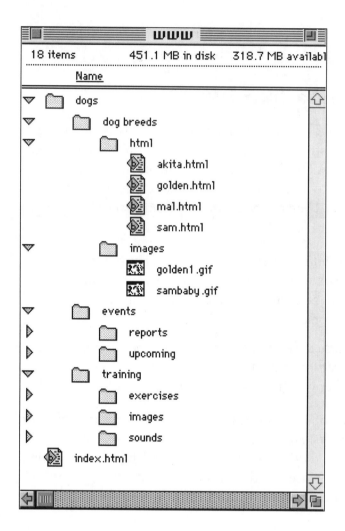

Figure 2.2
An orderly HTML file structure that makes it easy to find your site's files.

When creating a tag, separate each element—the tag name and switches—with a single space. If you forget to include the space, the browser will try to read the entire thing as one tag name and won't be able to process it.

You don't need to include a switch with the tags. If you don't use a switch, the browser just uses the default value for that tag. And not all tags have switches. For example, to turn text bold, you just enter the bold tag. There are no other options available.

To use a switch, type the switch name, an equals sign, and the switch value, as in the previous example. Don't put a space between the switch name, equals sign, or value. If the value is literal text or a value that is passed on to another function, surround it with quotation marks.

Tags are not case-sensitive. You can turn text bold by typing either <b> or <B>; both mean the same thing.

> **case-sensitive—** Recognizes the difference between uppercase and lowercase letters.

On and Off

Some tags stand alone. For example, you insert a graphic with a single image tag. Other tags create a state that stays in effect until you turn off the tag. For example, the bold command stays on until you turn it off.

To turn off a tag, precede the tag name with a slash. The following tags turn bold on and off:

```
<b>Bold Text</b>
```

TIP: *It's really important to remember to turn off tags. If you forget to turn off a tag, sometimes it is harmless and obvious that this is what you've done—your whole page appears bold. But other times, you'll just see a strange error—if you forget to turn off a table tag, for example, the rest of the document after the table seems to disappear.*

Basic File Structure

Using the same overall structure for your HTML files is important. Being consistent makes it easier to edit, debug, and update your files. Use extra returns to put white space in your text file. This makes your file easier to read.

TIP: *Remember, the HTML editor strips out extra spaces, so you aren't affecting the way the final page looks by adding extra returns, indents, or other spaces.*

UNDERSTANDING HTML

Here is a good, basic way to build an HTML file:

1. Start each file with a start-HTML tag. This tag tells the browser that the file contains HTML tags. The start-HTML tag looks like this:

   ```
   <html>
   ```

2. Next, create the heading section by typing the head tag like this:

   ```
   <head>
   ```

3. Set a title for the page. The title tag is one that you turn on and off. The value between the on and off tags is what appears in the title bar at the top of the browser window.

   ```
   <title>All About Animals</title>
   ```

4. If you want, enter some comments about the file. The comments might note when it was created or something you want to remember about it. Comments don't appear on the page; they are just in the file for your information. Any tag whose first character is the exclamation point (!) is treated as a comment.

   ```
   <! -- This is the first draft of the page.>
   ```

5. End the heading section.

   ```
   </head>
   ```

6. Put in a few returns to add some white space. Then, start the body section. The body is where the contents of your page go. Everything that appears after the body tag appears in your reader's browser.

   ```
   <body>
   ```

7. Create your page, typing text and tags as necessary.

8. At the end of the page, end the body section.

   ```
   </body>
   ```

9. Finally, type the end-HTML tag.

   ```
   </html>
   ```

Figure 2.3 shows a basic template and the page it generates.

To Each Its Own Line

In general, keep each tag on a separate line. This makes it easy to see what is going on. Codes don't become lost within a sea of text. The exceptions to this are in-body tags, such as the tag that makes a word bold, and the line-break command (<br>). The logical place for both of these are with the text they define.

TIP: *Just putting paragraph tags on a separate line makes your file much easier to read. The end page will look the same whether the tags are on the same line or a separate line, but your HTML file will be much cleaner with each paragraph tag on its own line. As a consequence, your file will be easier to edit.*

Ask yourself: In which of the files illustrated in Figure 2.4 is it easier to find the errors?

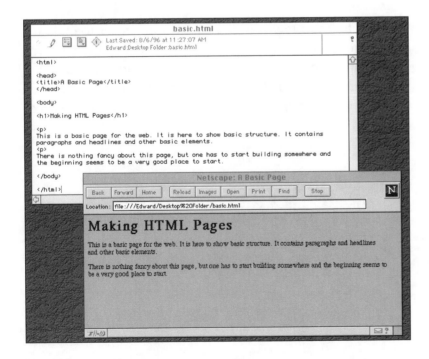

Figure 2.3
A basic HTML template and the page it creates.

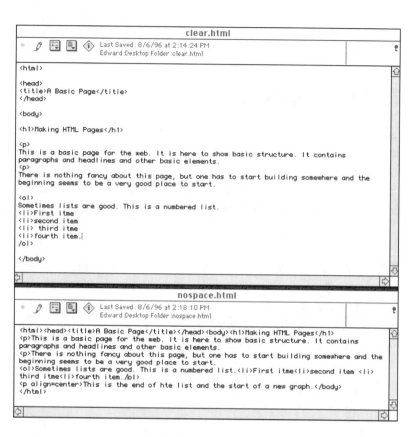

Figure 2.4
A neatly organized HTML file and a mishmash of HTML code. Both produce the same file, and both contain the same errors. Can you find the errors?

If you follow a few common-sense approaches to building your pages and organizing your files, you'll be putting down some solid cornerstones for all the future work that you do. Getting into good habits early is important, and, before you know it, you'll be creating clean files without thinking twice about it.

BASIC TEXT TAGS

The basic text tags let you build a simple HTML page and provide the platform for more complex pages. These tags let you break lines, create paragraphs, make headlines, and change the type's attributes.

> **attributes—**
> Characteristics.

As you read this chapter, you may want to go to the "Project Cool Teaches" Web site at http://www.projectcool. com/guide/html. There, you'll find the Try It section. In the Try It section, you can type in the examples and see how they look on the screen. There are also some practice exercises throughout this chapter. They'll look like this:

 TRY THIS: Try typing this in the Try It section.

As you learn about each of the tags, try typing the example in the text box to see how the different tags change the text's appearance. We can show you printed examples here in the book, but the effect is more memorable if you type the tags and see the results yourself.

To go to the Web site and use the Try It section:

1. Start the browser on your computer.

2. When the browser window appears, click in the location bar and delete the URL that you see there. The

location bar will be at the top left or bottom left of your screen, depending on the browser you are using.

3. With the cursor in the location bar, type

    `http://www.projectcool.com/guide/html`

4. Press the Return key.

5. The Try It section will appear in your browser window.

6. Follow the simple directions on the Try It screen to enter your example text and HTML tags.

 TRY THIS: Try this now to see how Try It works:

    1. Go to the Try It section in the browser.
    2. Click in the text window and type your name.
    3. Click on the Try It button.

Text without Tags

In its most simple form, an HTML file is text. This file:

```
Welcome to the Animals Page!
Click here to learn about the secret lives of animals.
```

displays like Figure 3.1 in a Web browser.

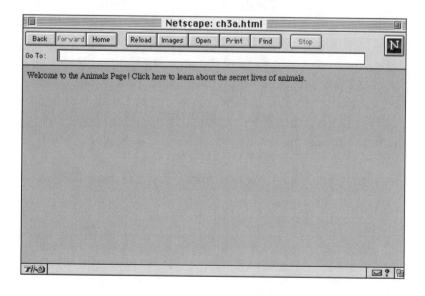

Figure 3.1
Raw text with no code in a browser window.

There are no tags to tell the browser to split the text. It just strings all the characters together in one long row.

The Break Tag (<br>)

The break tag tells the browser to display the text that follows it on a separate line. So, the file

```
Welcome to the Animals Page!<br>
Click here to learn about the secret lives of animals. <br>
```

displays like Figure 3.2 in a Web browser.

The Paragraph Tag (<p>)

The paragraph tag tells the browser to display the text that follows it on a separate line and to add extra space above it. So, the file

```
<p>
Welcome to the Animals Page!
<p>
Click here to learn about the secret lives of animals.
```

displays like Figure 3.3 in a Web browser.

**
**—Forces a new line in the page.

<p>—Forces a new line with a space before it.

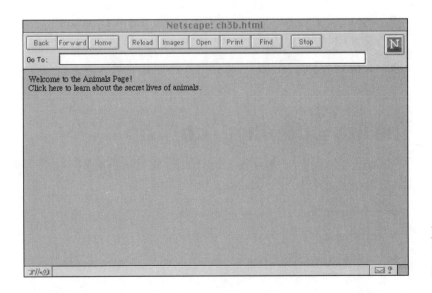

Figure 3.2
The effect of the break tag.

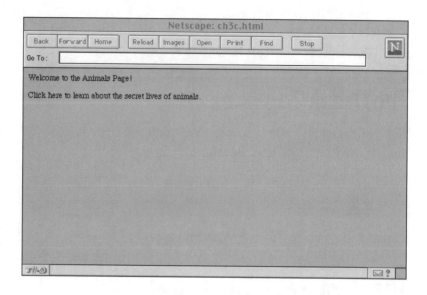

Back | Forward | Home | Reload | Images | Open | Print | Find | Stop

Go To :

Welcome to the Animals Page!

Click here to learn about the secret lives of animals.

Figure 3.3
The effect of the paragraph tag.

TIP: *Use the break tag when you want lines with no space between each line. Use the paragraph tag when you want lines with extra space in between or when you need to center or right-align the text. Notice that the paragraph tag is on a line by itself. This is a good file structure guideline to follow. It makes your HTML files easier to read.*

The paragraph tag has one switch: *align.* You can align text in three ways:

▶ *Left.* The default is left. If you don't use the align switch, the text automatically aligns to the left margin.

▶ *Right.* Type *<p align=right>* to send the text to the right margin.

▶ *Center.* Type *<p align=center>* to center the text across the page.

The Attribute Tags (<b/i/tt>)

The attribute tags tell the browser how to display the text that follows them. The text can be

▶ bold text

▶ italic text

▶ typewriter-style (monospaced) text

<b>—Sets text in bold.

<i>—Sets text in italic.

<tt>—Sets text in a typewriter-style, monospaced font.

CHAPTER 3

30

You can turn on multiple tags to create various combinations of bold, italic, and typewriter text. The attribute tags must be both turned on and turned off. They are always used in pairs.

TRY THIS:

1. Type a paragraph tag.
2. Type this line of text: *The big bold lion stares at the italic bars that surround him.*
3. Type another paragraph tag and an alignment switch, like this: *<p align= center>*
4. Type: *ROAR!*
5. Click TRY IT to see how the paragraphs look.
6. Move the cursor in front of the word *bold* and add the start-bold tag. Move to the end of the word and add the end-bold tag.
6. Add the italic start and end tags around the words *italic bars.*
7. Add both italic and bold tags around the *ROAR!* sentence. Remember to use start and end tags for both attributes.
8. Click on the Try It button to see how the attributes look. If you want, go back into the sentence and try adding additional start and end attribute tags to get a feel for how they work. Or change the alignment of the paragraphs.

TIP: *One common mistake is to accidentally have an on-tag in your file repeated twice. You happily type one off-tag and then wonder why all the text is still bold. What has happened is that each individual on-tag requires its own matching off-tag; you have two on-tags and only one off-tag, so the attribute doesn't turn off. Make sure each on-tag has a matching off-tag.*

<h1-6>—Displays headlines in levels 1 through 6.

The Headline Tag (<h1-6>)

For example, the file

```
<p align=center>
Welcome to the <b>Animals Page!</b>
<p align=center>
Click <b><i>here</i></b> to learn about the secret lives of animals.
```

displays like Figure 3.4 in a Web browser.

The headline tag tells the browser to display the text that follows it as a headline. There are six different levels of headlines, from H1 to H6. Some are bold; some are not. The size and attribute your reader sees depends on how his or her browser is set up.

Like the attribute tags, the headline tag must be turned on and turned off. For example:

```
<h1>Today's News!</h1>
```

Figure 3.5 shows examples of the different headline sizes; remember, the exact way they appear depends on your reader's browser settings.

Figure 3.4
The addition of paragraph align and attribute tags.

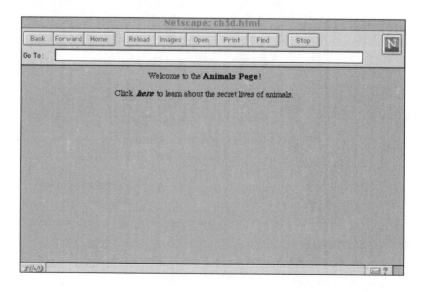

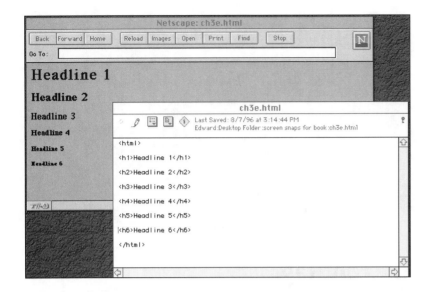

Figure 3.5
Headline tags and the way they appear in a browser window.

In general, you probably want to use only levels 1 through 3. If you find you need more than three headline levels, you may want to rethink how you have your page and information organized. Too many headline levels often means you're trying to fit too many levels of detail within the same general grouping.

Like the paragraph tag, the headline tag has one switch: *align.* And, like the paragraph tag, you can align text in three ways:

▶ *Left.* The default is left. If you don't use the align switch, the text automatically aligns to the left margin.

▶ *Right.* Type *<h1 align=right>* to send the text to the right margin.

▶ *Center.* Type *<h1 align=center>* to center the text across the page.

Here's an example of headline text in a file.

```
<h1 align=center>Welcome to the Animals Page!</h1>
<p align=center>
Click <b><i>here</i></b> to learn about the secret lives of animals.
```

The file displays like Figure 3.6 in a Web browser.

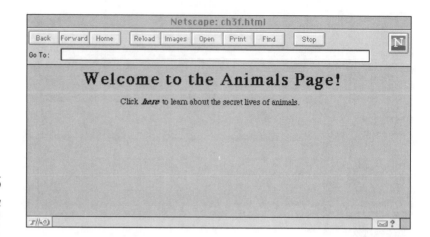

Figure 3.6
Headline tags within an HTML page.

Welcome to the Animals Page!

Click *here* to learn about the secret lives of animals.

The Font Tag
(<font size=+*x*/−*x* color="*xxx*">)

The font tag tells the browser to display the text that follows it at the specified size and/or color. Like the attribute tags, the font tag must be turned on and turned off.

The font tag has two switches: *size* and *color.*

► *Size.* The most common way to describe font size is in relation to the current size. You can tell the browser to set the type larger or smaller than the currently displayed size. So, if you want type that's a little bigger than the type around it, you'd type *<font size=+1>* To have type a little smaller than the type around it, you'd type *<font size=−1>.*

► *Color.* Colors are described by either name or hexadecimal number. The hexadecimal number describes the color as red, green, and blue color values. Appendix B shows the color names and hexadecimal numbers for a set of common colors. Because they are literal values, you must always surround the color name or hexadecimal number with quotation marks.

<font>—Controls font attributes, such as size and color, but not styles such as bold and italic.

hexadecimal number—Number expressed in base-16 notation. Very common in computer programming languages.

TIP: *You can create any color. There are utility programs that convert colors into hexadecimal numbers. You can find these utilities in*

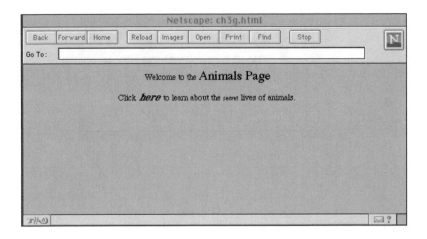

Figure 3.7
Font-size changes.

the Project Cool Developers zone (www.projectcool.com/developer) and in other locations across the Web. It is often easier, however, to use one of the standard, predefined colors that are supported on all computer platforms.

Here's an example of different font sizes.

```
<p align=center>
Welcome to the <font size=+2>Animals Page</font></h1>
<p align=center>
Click <b><i><font size=+1>here</font></i></b> to learn about
the <font size=-1>secret</font> lives of animals.
```

The file displays like Figure 3.7 in a Web browser.

TRY THIS:

1. Add a third line of text to the sentences you typed before:
   > The big bold lion stares at the italic bars that surround him.
   > ROAR!
   > growl . . .
2. Put the tag <font size=+2> in front of second line, and then end the font call by typing </font>. Put a tag <font size=-1> in front of the third, and then end the font call by typing </font> at the end of the line.

3. Click on TRY IT to see the results.
4. Now add some color. In front of the first line, type this tag: <font color="crimson">. Remember to end the font tag at the end of the line.
5. Click on TRY IT to see the results.
6. Play around with different sizes and colors. Look at Appendix B or open a new browser window to http://www.project-cool.com/developer/framed-ref-index.html to see a color reference guide.

Block-Quote Tag (<blockquote>)

The block-quote tag is a way of indenting a portion of your page. Like the attribute and font tags, you must remember to turn off the block-quote tag.

Here's an example of a block quote.

```
<h1 align=center>Welcome to the Animals Page!</h1>
<p align=center>
Click <b><i>here</i></b> to learn about secret lives of animals.
<blockquote>
There's more to animals than meets the eye. We'll take you inside
their hearts and minds and see what makes them tick. You'll never
look at animals quite the same again.
</blockquote>
```

This file displays like Figure 3.8 in a Web browser.

> **<blockquote>**—
> Used to inset a long quote within a text. Indents right and left margins of the text.

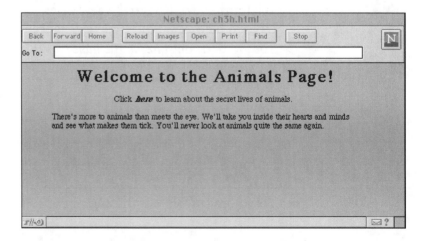

Figure 3.8
The blockquote tag in action.

TIP: *Notice that the block-quote and end-block-quote tags are on a line by themselves. This is a good file structure guideline to follow. It makes your HTML files easier to read.*

TRY THIS:

1. Type these three paragraphs. Put a paragraph tag in front of each.

   The myths of ancient civilizations continue to influence today's societies in ways both subtle and broad. One way we see it is in our language.

   "He's such a narcissus." "You'll be struck down by a bolt of lightning." "Marketing has always been that company's Achilles' heel."

   Mythological symbols also show up in logos, art, and design. Love it or hate it, there's just no escaping the fact that gods of old are still among us today.

2. Click on TRY IT.

3. Then, change the paragraph tag in front of the middle paragraph to a block-quote tag <blockquote> and end the paragraph with an end-block-quote tag </blockquote>.

4. Click on TRY IT to see the results.

MAKING LISTS

With HTML, you can create several kinds of lists.

Unordered lists are lists in which each item is preceded by a bullet of some sort. You can define the type of bullet you want to use. This is an unordered list:

▶ Tiger

▶ Lion

▶ Bear

bullet—Graphic at the beginning of a list item.

Ordered lists are lists in which each item is preceded by a number or letter. You can specify the starting number, as well as its style. This is an ordered list:

1. Open the door.

2. Pick up the trashbag.

3. Take out the trash.

Definition lists are lists in which a term is followed by an indented definition. This is a definition list:

Alpha

    The first letter in the ancient Greek alphabet. First, or primary.

Omega

    The last letter in the ancient Greek alphabet. Last, or end.

Each type of list works the same way.

1. You enter a tag that describes the type of list.

2. Then you tag each list item.

3. Finally, you end the list.

You can have paragraphs within lists. Paragraphs within a list are indented but are not preceded with a bullet or number.

You can also nest lists. That is, you can have lists within lists within lists.

nest—To embed one design element within another; also, something a bird builds.

TIP: *An easy-to-make mistake is to leave off the end-list tag. This leaves the list indent turned on, and the remainder of your page is indented. Make sure each of your lists has an end-list tag.*

Lists Should Be Legible

Lists, especially nested lists, are hotbeds for accidental errors. Keeping lists legible makes using them easier to debug. Here's a few tips for keeping the list tags orderly.

- *Keep tags on separate lines.* If your whole list runs together, you won't be able to tell where one piece stops and another one starts.

- *Consider adding an extra return to pull out lists visually.* Separating lists with white space makes them easier to find.

- *Indent nested lists.* Use the tab key to make a quick and easy indent. Remember, the browser ignores multiple spaces, so indenting in your ASCII text file won't affect the way the page displays.

Unordered Lists

To use an unordered list:

1. Type the unordered-list tag, <ul>.

2. On the next line, type a list-item tag, <li>.

3. Type the first list item.

4. On the next line, type another list-item tag, <li>. Then type the second list item.

5. When you reach the end of the list, type </ul>.

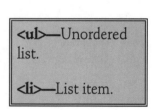

<ul>—Unordered list.

<li>—List item.

Here's an example of an unordered list.

```
<p>
In this section we look at the lives of three social animals:
<ul>
<li>Coyotes
<li>Lions
<li>Elephants
</ul>
```

This file displays like Figure 3.9 in a Web browser.

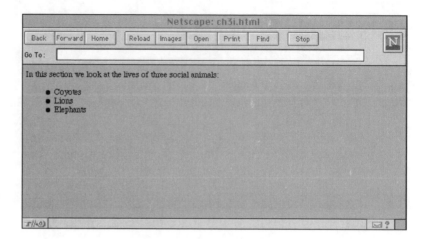

Figure 3.9
An unordered list.

You can specify the type of bullet you want to use by adding the type switch. You can put the switch in the start-list (<ul type=square>) to set a specific bullet for the entire list. Or, you can put the switch in a list-item tag (<li type= circle>) to use a specific bullet for that list item only.

There are three types of bullet settings: *disc* (●), *circle* (○), and *square* (□).

▶ *Disc* is the default, generating a solid circle (<ul type=disc>).

▶ *Circle* is a hollow circle (<ul type=circle>).

▶ *Square* is a hollow box (<ul type=square>).

 TRY THIS:

1. Create an unordered list with these six items: Baseball cap, Top hat, Beret, Felt derby, Terrycloth visor, Knit stocking cap. Remember to start and end the list with start <ul> and end </ul> tags.
2. Click TRY IT to see the result.
3. Edit the tag <li> to add a type switch. Set the first two items with a disc bullet, the second two with a square bullet, and the final two with a circle bullet.
4. Click TRY IT again to see the changes.

Ordered Lists

To use an ordered list:

1. Type the ordered-list tag, <ol>.

2. On the next line, type a list-item tag, <li>.

3. Type the first list item.

4. On the next line, type another list-item tag, <li>. Then type the second list item.

5. When you reach the end of the list, type the end-ordered-list tag, </ol>.

Here's an example of an ordered list.

```
In this section we look at the lives of three social animals:
<ol>
<li>Coyotes
<li>Lions
<li>Elephants
</ol>
```

The file above displays like Figure 3.10 in a Web browser.

The ordered list has two switches. Like the unordered-list switches, the ordered-list switches can go into either the start-ordered-list tag or an individual list-item tag.

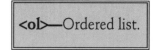

<ol>—Ordered list.

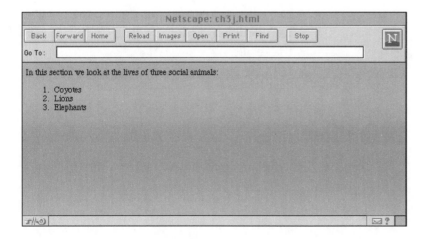

Figure 3.10
An ordered list.

The type switch lets you specify whether to use numbers or letters in your ordered list. The default value is Arabic numerals.

▶ The tag <ol type=I> produces a numerical list with roman numerals.

▶ The tag <ol type=i> produces a numerical list with small roman numerals.

▶ The tag <ol type=A> produces an alphabetical list with capital letters.

▶ The tag <ol type=a> produces a alphabetical list with lowercase letters.

▶ The tag <ol type=1> produces a numerical list with Arabic numerals. This is also the default value. If you don't enter a type switch, the list will use Arabic numerals.

The start switch lets you start the ordered list at a specific number. For example:

```
<ol start=15>
```

starts the list with the number 15.

TRY THIS:

1. Use the same list of hats from the previous example—Baseball cap, Top hat, Beret, Felt derby, Terrycloth visor, Knit stocking cap—but change the unordered tags (<ul>) to ordered tags (<ol>). Click TRY IT to see the result.
2. Edit the tag <ol> to add a type=A switch and click TRY IT again to see the changes.

Definition Lists

The definition list displays items in two parts. The first is a definition term. The second is an indented definition description.

To use a definition list:

1. Type the definition-list tag, <dl>.

2. On the next line, type a definition-term tag, <dt>

3. Type the first term.

4. On the next line, type the definition-description tag, <dd>. Then type the term's definition.

5. When you read the end of the list, type the end-definition-list tag, </dl>.

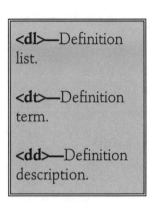

<dl>—Definition list.

<dt>—Definition term.

<dd>—Definition description.

Here's an example of a definition list.

```
<dl>
<dt>Coyotes
<dd>The prankster of Indian lore, the bane of urban life, but
really a relative of the dog with a complex social structure.
<dt>Lions
<dd>The male lion may have the mane of legend, but the female
runs the pride.
<dt>Elephants
<dd>Highly intelligent, they develop life-long relationships
and may even mourn for their dead.
</ol>
```

This file displays like Figure 3.11 in a Web browser.

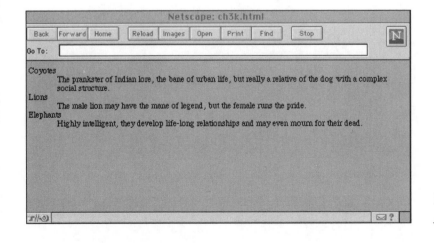

Figure 3.11
A definition list.

TIP: *You can use definition lists for more than pure terms and definitions. They can be a useful formatting tool any time you want a word or phrase followed by an indented word or phrase.*

TRY THIS:
Enter the following as a definition list. Click on Try It to see the results. Remember to end the list!

> *Baseball cap*
>> *Wool or cotton. In 10 team logos. Or custom-order your own logo.*
>
> *Top hat*
>> *A classic look in black or white silk.*
>
> *Beret*
>> *How continental! In hunter green, deep blue, or timeless noir.*

Nested Lists

> **nested lists**—Lists within lists.

You can create lists within lists, combining different types of lists to create the effect you want.

TIP: *When you nest lists, make sure you use extra white space and indents in your file to make it readable. And be sure to turn off each list. An easy-to-make mistake is to forget to turn off one of the nested lists.*

Here's an example of nested lists. The file

```
<ol>
<li>Coyotes
    <ol type=A>
    <li>Eastern
    <li>Western
    </ol>
<li>Lions
<li>Elephants
    <ol type=A>
    <li>Asian
    <li>African
    </ol>
</ol>
```

displays like Figure 3.12 in a Web browser.

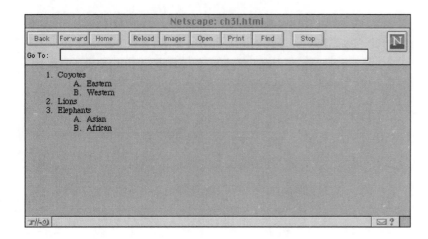

Netscape: ch3l.html

| Back | Forward | Home | | Reload | Images | Open | Print | Find | | Stop | |

Go To:

1. Coyotes
    A. Eastern
    B. Western
2. Lions
3. Elephants
    A. Asian
    B. African

Figure 3.12
Nested lists.

TRY THIS: Create a series of nested lists, using the following example. Click on TRY IT when you are done. Remember to end each list!

1. The top-level list, which contains the hat and hat description, is a definition list.
2. The nested lists, which list the color options, are unordered lists.

Baseball cap

>   *Wool or cotton. In 10 team logos. Or custom-order your own logo.*
>   - *Red*
>   - *Navy*
>   - *White*

Top hat

>   *A classic look in black or white silk.*
>   - *Classic black*
>   - *Classic white*

Beret

>   *How continental!*
>   - *Hunter green*
>   - *Deep blue*
>   - *Timeless noir*

Now that you have seen the basics, try creating your own simple page. Many people start out with a personal home page. It can be very elementary, with just your name and some notes about your work or your pets or your hobbies. Later on you can add images, links, and more complex formatting. The only way to really learn to build the Web is to create actual pages. Go ahead—give it a go!

4

CREATING LINKS

Most of the media we know are linear. You start watching or reading in one place and follow through paragraphs and scenes in a specific order. There is a clear beginning, middle, and end. Not only is there a beginning, middle, and end, but the flow from one to the next is determined by the creator of the content. You put one paragraph first, follow it with a quote, and end with a pithy comment. Your reader reads your work as you present it.

In the Web medium, there is a different dynamic at work. The Web is a nonlinear medium. Linking together different ideas and content is the core strength of the Web. Although it is important to provide a possible path for your readers, the readers are really the ones in control. They decide where they want to begin, follow links to explore ideas that interest them, and eventually reach an endpoint that makes sense for them. If they are forced to follow a strict preset path, they will quite often go elsewhere.

For the content creator, this can feel a little scary. It is as if the order of the universe is flipped on its head—how can people read my work the right way? There is no absolute right way on the Web, but using the power of links wisely is one way of drawing on the inherent strength of the Web medium.

HTML tags let you provide seamless links between sets of information. With a simple click, your reader can jump to another location in your site or to another site elsewhere on the Web or on the Internet. You can link to actions as well, creating a spot on your page where people can click to send you e-mail or download a software update you're offering. When we use the word *link,* we are referring to both content and action links.

This chapter teaches you how to create links and provides some ideas for building multidirectional paths into your design.

PUTTING LINKS IN YOUR HTML

Within your HTML page you can create a link to:

▶ A spot within your current file

▶ Another file on your server

▶ Any file on a WWW server

▶ A file you want people to download onto their own computer

▶ An e-mail form that sends e-mail to a specified address

▶ A file on a gopher server

▶ A file on a WAIS server

▶ A file on a Usenet newsgroup

▶ A Telnet connection to a server

To set a link, you'll use the HTML anchor tag.

The Anchor Tag <a>

You can use the anchor tag to make either a portion of text or a graphic become a link on which people can click. The anchor tag tells the browser to set a hypertext link for the designated text or graphic. The text will usually appear in a highlighted color to indicate that it represents a link. The graphic may have a colored box around it, or the graphic itself may simply be something that looks button-like or clickable. When a reader clicks on the link, the browser performs the action specified in the anchor tag.

Like the attribute tags, the anchor tag must be both turned on and turned off. In the ASCIII HTML file, the text or graphic that is linked appears between the on and off tags. The anchor tag describes the linked file or action by its Uniform Resource Locator—its URL. The URL describes the type of file and the file's location by resource type, server, and filename.

Uniform Resource Locator (URL)—Way of describing a file on the Internet.

Figure 4.1 shows an example of what a link looks like in a Web browser. Note that the link itself is underlined (or set in a color) to indicate that something more is there. The highlighted text indicates a link. When your readers click on it, they go to the file described by that link or see the action described by the link.

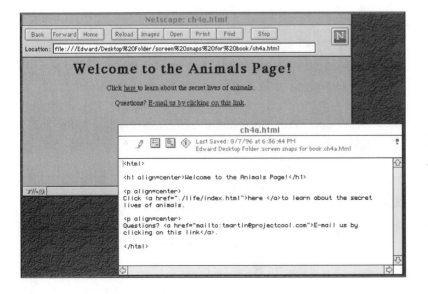

Figure 4.1
An HTML page with two links. The first brings up another page; the second lets the reader send e-mail to the page's creator.

Setting a Link: The Basics

Here's how to set the most basic type of link in your HTML file:

1. Put the cursor in front of the text or graphic that will act as the link.

2. Type the anchor tag.

   ```
   <a
   ```

3. Type a space.

4. Type the href switch and an equals sign (*href* stands for "hypertext reference").

   ```
   <a href=
   ```

5. Type a quotation mark, the URL to which you want to link, and another quotation mark.

   ```
   <a href="http://www.projectcool.com"
   ```

6. Close the tag.

   ```
   <a href="http://www.projectcool.com">
   ```

7. Move to the end of the linked text or graphic and type an end-anchor tag.

   ```
   <a href="http://www.projectcool.com">Go to Project Cool</a>
   ```

TIP: *One easy-to-make error in creating an anchor tag is to leave off one of the quotation marks around the URL. If one of the quotation marks is missing, the browser ignores the entire area with the anchor tag, and it seems that part of your file has just disappeared. Make sure the URL starts with a quote and ends with a quote.*

TRY THIS:
1. Go to the Try It section.
2. Type the words: *Linking is easy. This sentence links to Project Cool's home page.*

3. Put the cursor in front of the second sentence and create a link to http://www.projectcool.com.
4. Go to the end of the sentence and end the anchor tag.
5. Click on TRY IT. Click on your newly created link and see what happens.

Linking to a Specific Spot in a File

Normally, a linked file opens at the beginning. It's like pulling a book of the shelf and opening to the front page. However, you can also mark a specific place in a file and tell the browser to open to that exact location. This is like putting a bookmark on page 101, where the definition of *spots* is found, so that you can automatically flip to it every time.

There are lots of ways you can use this feature. For example, you could send people to a glossary definition in the middle of another file. Or, you could create a miniature table of contents at the beginning of your file and, with links, let people jump to other places within the same file. Linking to a specific spot can help your links make better logical sense.

TIP: *If your file is very long, you might want to consider breaking it into small files that you can link together. Often, when people make the transition from print to the Web, they forget that they can break long files into smaller, linked ones. Smaller files load faster over a modem.*

As shown in Figure 4.2, there are two steps to linking to a specific location:

1. First, you create an anchor mark at the precise spot to which you want to link.

2. Then, you create the link to the anchored place using the anchor tag.

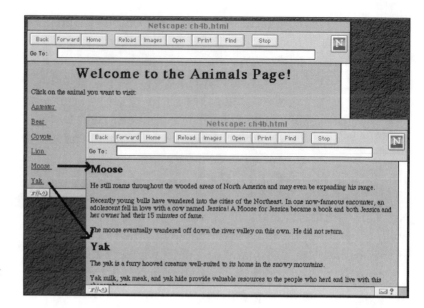

Figure 4.2
Linking to a specific location within a file.

To link to a specific spot:

1. Open the file to which you want to link and move the cursor to the spot you want to mark. This is what will appear in the browser window after your click on the link.

2. Type the anchor tag.

    <a

3. Type a space.

4. Type the *name* switch followed by the equals sign.

    <a name=

5. Then type the name you want to give this mark. Make sure you enclose it in quotes. The name must be one word without any spaces.

    <a name="gohere"

6. Close the tag.

    <a name="gohere">

7. Now, go to your HTML file and start to make the link as you normally would: Start the anchor tag, and then type the URL of the file that contains the mark.

8. Instead of ending the anchor tag here, type a pound sign (#) and the name you gave the anchor mark.

```
<a
href="http://www.projectcool.com/examples/anchors.html#gohere">
```

9. Close the tag and type the end-anchor tag as usual.

Making an E-mail Link

One kind of link that can be especially useful is a Send E-mail function. When your readers click on the link, they'll see a box where they can type a message. The e-mail is automatically sent to the address you specify in the link.

To make an e-mail link:

1. Put the cursor in front of the text or graphic that will act as the link.

2. Type the anchor tag.

```
<a
```

3. Type a space.

4. Type *href* and an equal sign.

```
<a href=
```

5. Type a quotation mark followed by *mailto:*

```
<a href="mailto:
```

6. Type the e-mail address to which you want your readers to send their message.

```
<a href="mailto:tmartin@projectcool.com
```

7. Type a quote and close the tag.

```
<a href="mailto:tmartin@projectcool.com">
```

8. Move to the end of the linked text or graphic and type an end-anchor tag.

 TRY THIS:

1. Go to the Try It and type the words: *Questions? Send an e-mail to us by clicking HERE.*
2. Use the font tag to make the word HERE two sizes larger than the surrounding text.
3. Add an e-mail link to the word HERE. Try sending a message to this address: guide@projectcool.com (*Hint:* <a href= "mailto:guide@projectcool.com">—and don't forget to end the anchor tag!).
4. Click on TRY IT. Click on your newly created link and see what happens.

Letting Your Readers Download a File

Another kind of link you can make is to a "transfer file" function. When your readers click on the link, the file you specify will begin to download from your server to their local computer. In this case, the file is most often stored on an FTP server. FTP stands for File Transfer Protocol and is a means of transmitting files over the Internet.

Some people use the Web to let their customers download software updates or demo software or to get a product brochure or a report. All the customer has to do is click on the text or graphic link, and the file transfer begins automatically.

TIP: *If your readers will be downloading a file, talk to your ISP to be sure the Web server is configured to handle downloading that type of file.*

To make a file transfer link:

1. Put the cursor in front of the text or graphic that will act as the link.

2. Type the anchor tag.

```
<a
```

3. Type a space.

4. Type *href* and an equals sign.

```
<a href=
```

5. Type a quotation mark, then type *ftp://*

```
<a href="ftp://
```

6. Type the server name and the path to the file you want your readers to download.

```
<a href="ftp://ftp.projectcool.com/pub/demofile.txt
```

7. Type a quote and close the tag.

```
<a href=" ftp://ftp.projectcool.com/pub/demofile.txt">
```

8. Move to the end of the linked text or graphic and type an end-anchor tag.

MORE ABOUT URLs

The Uniform Resource Locator describes a file by type and location. Figure 4.3 shows how a URL is structured.

Resource type describes the file protocol of the file. For example, a file on a WWW server uses the hypertext transfer protocol, http. A mail resource has the resource type mailto.

resource type— The Internet protocal of a file or action, such as http or mailto.

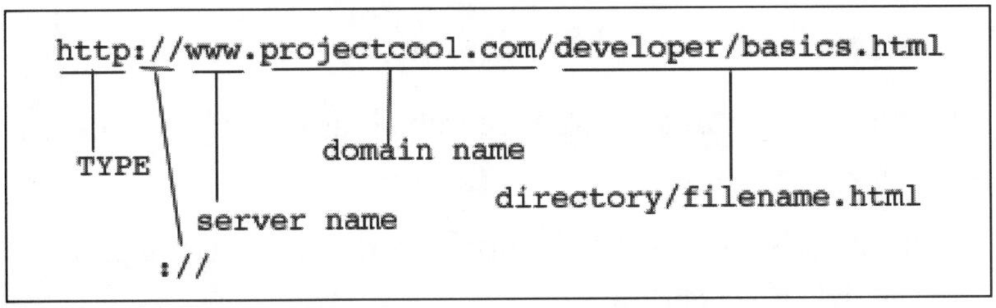

```
http://www.projectcool.com/developer/basics.html

    TYPE            domain name
                                    directory/filename.html
            server name
        ://
```

Figure 4.3
Basic URL structure.

▶ The type is followed with a colon and two slashes.

▶ Server name is the name of the computer on which the file resides. Often, you'll see the server described as "www" for World Wide Web. Using this name is a convention; not everyone does this. Some people leave it out entirely.

▶ The server type is followed by a period.

▶ The domain name is the World Wide Web address of the computer.

The filename is the name of the file. Sometimes the URL points to a specific file. Other times it points to a directory. When it points to a directory, the Web browser will automatically pull up your index file.

TIP: *Each directory in your Web site should have a file named "index.html" that is a sort of master guide to items within the directory.*

Resource File Types

There are several types of files your Web browser can see and that you can link to in your own HTML pages. They are:

▶ *http.* Hypertext Transfer Protocol. This describes a file on a World Wide Web server.

▶ *mailto.* E-mail. This starts a process of creating an e-mail message to the designated recipient.

▶ *ftp.* File transfer protocol. This starts a process of downloading a specified file.

▶ *gopher.* This describes a file on a gopher server.

▶ *wais.* Wide area internet search. This describes a file on a WAIS server.

▶ *news.* Usenet News Group. This describes a file on a Usenet news server.

---

index file—The main file in each of your Web site directories that connects all the other files.

http—Hypertext Transfer Protocol.

mailto—Starts a process of creating an e-mail message.

gopher—File on a gopher server. A gopher server is a way of arranging textual information on the Internet.

wais—Wide area internet search.

news—Usenet News Group, a file on a Usenet news server.

▶ *telnet.* This opens a computer connection to the specified server and lets you enter commands as if you were logged onto that server.

To link to any of these resource types, just enter the resource type and the filename after the href switch in the anchor text. For example, to link to a file on a gopher server, your link would look like this:

```
<a href="gopher://gopher.micro.umn.edu:70/1/">
```

Ways of Describing URLs

The URL you saw in Figure 4.3 is the fully expanded URL. That means it is described by its complete name, including resource type. This is what you'd type into a Web browser to go to that file.

When you are linking to a URL in your HTML page, you can use the fully expanded URL. In fact, if you're describing a file someplace on the Web outside your site, you'll always use a full URL. But, if your links are within your site, you'll want to use relative links. Relative links describe the linked file's location in relation to the current file.

TIP: *Relative linking makes your site "transportable." If you need to move your Web site, you don't have to go back in and change all your links as you would if you had used fully expanded links. Try to use relative linking wherever possible.*

Describing Relative Links

To use relative links, you need to be familiar with a little basic UNIX file directory notation and the way the browser looks for files. File directory notation is way the computer uses symbols, like slashes and periods, to describe the location of a file.

---

telnet—Telnet connection, a type of Interent connection that logs you onto a remote server.

fully expanded URLs—URLs called by their complete filename, including resource type (i.e., http://www.project-cool.com).

relative links—URLs called in a way that indicates their relative placement within a local file system.

file-directory notation—The way a computer uses symbols to describe a file's storage location.

Slashes

The slash symbol by itself tells the browser to look for the file in the root directory. The root directory is the first-level directory on the computer.

When used at the beginning of a filename, the slash symbol acts like a "return to go." For example, *<a href="/filename">* tells the browser to go the root directory to find the specified file. The slash symbol is also used to separate directories and subdirectories. When used in the middle of a filename, the slash symbol is a divider. For example, *<a href="/dogs/akita.html">* tells the browser to go the "dogs" directory to find the specified file, akita.html.

Periods (or dots)

The dot-dot symbol says to go up one directory level. It is a "take-one-step-back" symbol. For example, *<a href="../dogs/akita.html">* tells the browser to back up one directory level, and then find the "dogs" directory and go to the specified file, akita.html.

The browser reads a filename from left to right, in the same way that the English-speaking world reads text.

Here's the process it uses:

1. The browser "sees" the filename. The first place it looks for that file is in the current directory. No file there? Well . . .

2. It then goes back and looks at the filename. Is there a slash? If there is a slash, it jumps immediately to the root directory and looks for the file there. No slash? Well . . .

3. It might see dots. If it sees two dots, it backs up one directory level and looks for the file there. Not there either? Well . . .

4. Maybe the dots are followed by a slash. That means to enter the specified subdirectory and look for the file

there. Still can't find it? The server throws up its metaphorical arms and gives you a "File not found" error message.

DESIGNING FOR A NONLINEAR MEDIUM

Have you thought about how you use the Web? Many people say they "surf the Web" or go "Web surfing," comparing browsing the Web to riding a wave and steering a surfboard. That's a nice image and a nice phrase, but, in reality, browsing the Web is probably a bit more like burrowing or tunneling. That's because you're not really riding on the surface of anything but finding paths through the middle of something, much like an earthworm does. You have to assume, though, that they couldn't call it World Wide Worms—that's not a very attractive image. Surfing sounds a lot more inviting.

In either case, it's a nonlinear world. Neither burrowers nor surfers follow a clear path from *A* to *B*. The people who read your Web pages don't, either. The trick in designing a Web site is to find the right balance between showing people a path and giving them room to explore. The right balance will also vary depending on what your site is all about—if it is primarily searchable content, the design and the way items are linked will be quite different than if it is an electronic novel.

Editing is *not* a dirty word. One of the things your site does is present information to people in an orderly manner. Editing adds value. It makes the information easier to use and lets people feel satisfied as they find things that interest them or information that they need. There's a myth out there that says what people want from the Internet is unedited, unfettered data. If that were true, the Web would never have gained the popularity it has. What the Web adds is design, structure, and editing capabilities. These aren't constraints but tools for communication.

What follows are a few rules of thumb that we've found work well. If you think about these things as you create links and paths through your site, using your site will be a better experience for your reader.

The 30-Second Rule

Within 30 seconds of selecting your page, your readers should be able to download the page and understand what to do next. This means using technology and design decisions to minimize file size and structuring a page such that buttons and navigational guides are clear and understandable.

▶ Make sure your page has links, buttons, arrows, menus, or some other clear directional device. It is better to be obvious than clever. If readers have to puzzle out what to do next, they'll move on to some other site.

▶ Remember than many of your readers might be using a 14-inch monitor. Buttons, arrows, and menu choices at the bottom of a deep page are invisible to these readers until they scroll. It is best to have some navigational guide "above the fold"; that is, in the portion of the page that appears on a 14-inch computer screen.

▶ If you want people to do something, tell them so. For example, sometimes people design first pages that contain just one big graphic. Click on the page, and you enter the site. But not everyone knows that clicking is a option. It's a good idea to include a line of text that says, "Click anywhere on the page to continue."

▶ Look at the chapter on low bandwidth for some ideas on creating nice, tight files that download quickly without sacrificing visual impact.

Rule of Fives

For reasons we don't fully understand, the human brain is designed to process information in chunks. Look at Figure 4.4. How many Saturns do you see?

Figure 4.4
How many Saturns?

Now look at Figure 4.5. How many Saturns are there?

In the first figure, you most likely saw all five Saturns simultaneously. But in the second, your brain mostly likely divided the Saturns into two groups and then added them together, or actually counted the number.

A set of five is the maximum number of items an average person can see as one unit. Put five pennies on the table, and, at a glance, anyone can tell you there are five. Put six pennies on the table, and people have to count or divide them into smaller groups—for example, two threes equal six. And remember, we have five fingers on our hand—one nice unit of five.

What does this means for designing a Web site? Try to limit the options you offer on any page to five. If you have more than five options on a page, people either begin to get confused or they never read all the options.

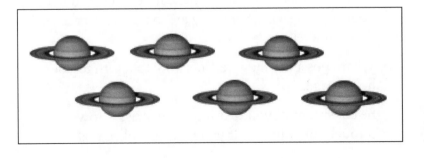

Figure 4.5
How many Saturns?

Three-Level Parking

When people travel though linked information, they build a mental map of where they've been and where they want to go. And they get frustrated if they have to keep digging and digging to get to the information that they want. A good rule of thumb to use in site design is that readers should never have to travel more than three mouse clicks to reach the information they want within your site.

Try applying the three-click rule within a site, not just from the home page. In our site, for example, if you are in Sightings, it is only three clicks to reach Coolest. If you are in Coolest, it is only three clicks to reach Developer's Zone. If you are on the home page, it is less than three clicks to reach a Future Focus article.

Like five options, three levels is a comfortable chunk for most people to track in their mind. And by keeping mouse clicks to a minimum, you satisfy your readers quickly, which encourages them to return.

Use Roadsigns

Provide navigational aids to make using your site easier.

- ▶ Let readers know where they can go next. Make the clickable options clear and understandable. Sometimes words are better than icons because there is no mistaking what they mean.

- ▶ Let readers know where they are now. Put a meaningful name in the title bar, or make it obvious through your page design where they are in relation to the rest of the site.

- ▶ Where possible, show readers how to return to your home page.

- ▶ Be consistent. If you're using arrows, use arrows throughout your site. If you're using linked text to navigate, use linked text throughout your site. Part of good navigation is setting up rules that are easy for your readers to learn and follow.

▶ Be obvious. It is better for your readers to be able to use your site than to marvel over how clever you are in creating a complex navigation scheme.

Don't Weave Chainmail

Don't overuse links. Linking is cool and can add great value. Because it is so cool and it is also so easy to do, there's a great temptation to link everything. Don't.

▶ Like other design elements, use links to add value to the content. Ask yourself: Would I follow this link? Would it be worth my while to follow this link? Does following this link add to my message or send me off on a tangent—an interesting tangent, but a tangent none the less?

▶ One way to think about links is to compare them to sidebars in printed media. A link is generally appropriate where a sidebar would be.

▶ Linking every word of text to something else is overkill and can be confusing to read. It's hard to follow a stream of thought when every other word is screaming, "Click on me!"

5

INCORPORATING IMAGES

Whether they are used as illustrations on a page, as background, or as links, images add style and pizzazz to a site. They're fun, they get people's attention, and they are one of the strengths of the Web.

Of course, they also add overhead and download time, and lots of Web sites have images because, well, just because they can. When you're building your site, use images well and with care. Your site will look better, and your readers (especially those with modems) will thank you for it.

This chapter talks about the mechanics of adding images to your Web page, both within the page and as a background. It also gives you some tips for selecting and preparing an image in a way that will work well on a computer screen.

You can also turn an image into an imagemap. An imagemap lets you create multiple clickable areas on an image. Imagemaps are covered in detail in Chapter 7. Before using imagemaps, though, you should feel comfortable working with straight images.

PREPARING AN IMAGE FOR THE WEB

Just as you do with other media, use graphics with thought for the value they bring. Just putting graphics on the page for the sake of graphics is never a good idea. If you can think of no reason to have a graphic where you are thinking of putting one, then don't put one there. Use graphics appropriately and not arbitrarily.

One of the most important things to remember about putting graphics in your Web site is that people will be viewing them on a computer screen. Most of us are used to thinking about how things look on paper, and we bring along a lot of those assumptions to the computer screen. But there are some very big differences.

Not All Monitors Are the Same

When you prepare an image for printing, the final product will be presented in the same way to all readers. Maybe it is a two-column-by-five-inch photo in a glossy magazine. Or maybe it is an 8-x-10 laser color print. Whatever it is, all the readers will see it on the same kind of paper, printed with the same kind of ink. That's not at all true in an image for a Web site.

There are a myriad of monitors out there. Just because something looks wonderful on your particular monitor is no guarantee that the colors will be just as sharp on someone else's monitor. For designers, this is a common trap, because they typically work with nice, large, high-end displays. The average reader doesn't.

All displays share a common set of colors. If a color in your image doesn't fall into one of these colors and if the reader's display doesn't support your particular color, then it will interpolate it into the closest possible match. Early on, we chose a lovely bright gold for links from one of our sections. Readers with older color displays on PCs quickly let us know that they couldn't read any text in that color. Oops, we forgot our own basic rules!

Photographic images often have colors that are not supported by the display. And different displays are adjusted differently by their users. That's one of the reasons photos sometimes look muddy or washed out on a Web site—they were probably optimized for the creator's display at its brightness and contrast settings.

If you can, it is a good idea to look at your pages on a couple different computers before you release them to the world. You'll be surprised at how quickly your notions of consistency change.

Another difference can occur between Macintosh and PC displays that are set to 8-bit (256-color) modes. The palettes on these machines are different and only share 216 colors. We've made available on our Web site a GIF image of this palette. It can be found at http://www.projectcool.com/guide/html/images/palette.gif.

> **palette**—A set of available colors.

Like everything else on the Web, think about your audience. If your readership is "anyone with a home computer," don't make assumptions about the way your images will appear. It is likely that your audience is still mostly using 256-color displays, so take that into account as you design your Web graphics. But if you know that most of your readers will be on SGI Indys, then by all means design for that nice, clear monitor.

We'll admit that we are sometimes color snobs. Here at Project Cool we often create our graphics in 24-bit color with little regard for the 216-color palette. You will notice that there are many sites on the Web that do so also. This is because of the increasing use of true-color graphics displays. These displays are beginning to appear at all levels of the computer market. A large portion of our audience falls into the category of people who are mostly using true-color displays, so, for us, it makes sense to create for these displays. If you think your audience is using true color, you should certainly design in that mode.

And then there are some people out there who design for the sixteen colors of the original PC palette. This is definitely not cool!

Resolution

resolution—The number of pixels per inch.

antialiasing— A technique that makes fonts look smoother, as if they are displayed at a higher resolution.

In print, we've all learned about the importance of high resolution for good reproduction. On the Web, forget it. Most monitors display images at 72 dpi. It doesn't matter how much data you have crammed into the image file—the limiting factor is that computer screen. But that's actually a good thing. You can get some very nice results from reasonably sized files at 72 dpi. For example, photos you take with an Apple QuickTake or other basic electronic camera don't look particularly sharp when you print them on your home color printer . . . but on a Web site, they can shine.

This is also where you can take advantage of features of programs such as Photoshop. For example, using fonts on the Web is something that is currently done via graphics. (HTML offers a rather limited selection of typewriter- or not-typewriter-type styles.) If you're using fonts, be sure to take advantage of antialiasing. Antialiasing is a technique in which pixels of varying shades between the foreground and background colors are used to smooth out the edges of a line and eliminate the stairstep or jaggy effect that you often seen in type that is not antialiased. Antialiasing lets you simulate a higher resolution and can produce much more professional-looking graphics. Figure 5.1 shows the

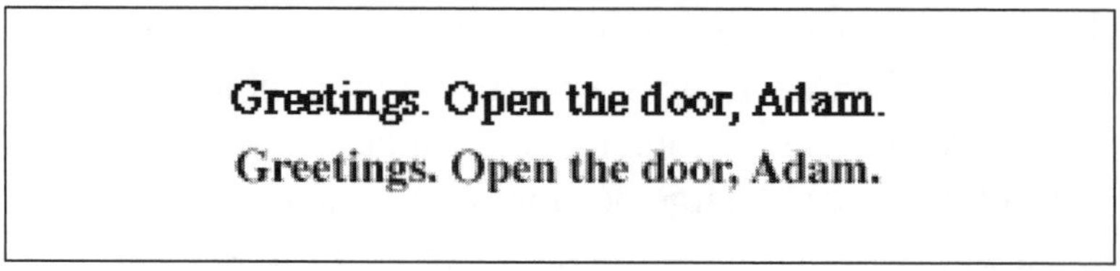

Figure 5.1
Type without antialiasing (top); the same text with antialiasing (bottom).

Greetings. Open the door, Adam.
Greetings. Open the door, Adam.

difference between a bare-naked graphic and one that has been antialiased.

File Size

The size of your final file is a very important factor in Web design. It's pretty silly to have a file that takes many, many minutes to download on a modem, yet it's amazing how many sites out there will do just that. Here's a good rule of thumb to remember: It takes one second per K of file to transfer over a modem.

For example, if you had a 30K graphics file, it would take 30 seconds to download over a 14.4 modem. Is your audience going to sit still for 30 seconds just to see one picture? We'll be discussing some techniques to help cut down on file size in Chapter 9.

A Few Basic Tips

Here's a few basic tips to get you started. (For more detailed information on creating low-bandwidth graphics, see Chapter 9.)

▶ In general, save files with a limited palette and/or large areas of solid color in GIF format. This includes most line art and graphics that you create with a drawing program.

▶ In general, save files with a wide palette in JPEG format. This includes most photographs and other photorealistic images. Early Web browsers treated JPEG as a file type that required a separate helper application, but JPEG support is integrated into all the recent versions of the major browsers.

▶ For most images, use the number of bits that your graphic program offers as a default for that image. Photoshop, for example, will calculate the number of colors in an image and, when you save, will display the best option.

- For most JPEG images, medium quality is acceptable.

- Keep in mind that, as a designer, you are much more finicky about the finished image than your audience. The average user will never notice the one pixel that you feel is just slightly off in your image. Learn when to let go and to accept a quality that may not always be up to your exacting standards or discerning eye.

PUTTING AN IMAGE INTO YOUR PAGE

<img>—Inserts an image.

The process of adding images is quite straightforward. You add them with the image tag, <img>. The image tag tells the browser to display a specific image at this point in the page. There is no off-image tag. For example, the HTML code in Figure 5.2 creates the HTML page you see directly above it.

The image tag has six basic switches:

- *Source (src).* This is the location and name of the image you are using. As with anchors and links, use the full URL if the image is on another server. Use relative

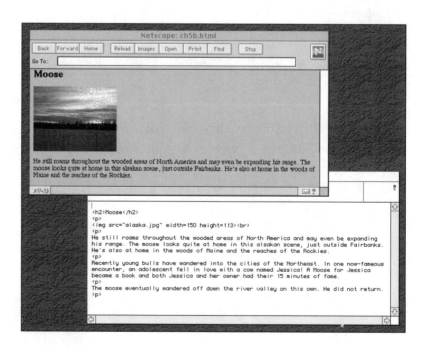

Figure 5.2
An image within an HTML page.

URLs if it's within your own site. Remember that the URL must begin and end with quotes.

▶ *Alignment (align).* You can align the image to the right or left side of the page. You cannot center it.

TIP: *If you want to center an image, try this trick: Put a center-aligned paragraph tag above the image.*

▶ *Width.* Width of the image in pixels.

▶ *Height.* Height of the image in pixels.

▶ *Border.* Width of the border around the image in pixels when the image is used as a hypertext link. You need only set this switch when the image is also the anchor for a link.

▶ *Alternate text (alt).* This is the text that appears in a reader's browser if the reader has his or her image loading turned off or if the browser doesn't display graphics. You usually want to include some brief alternate text so that those readers know what the image represents. Remember that the text must be surrounded with quotation marks.

To insert an image with the image tag:

1. Go to the location in your HTML file where you want the image to appear.

2. Type the image tag

```
<img
```

3. Add the name of the image with the source switch. Remember to enclose the image's name in quotes.

```
<img src="images/dog1.gif"
```

4. Add other switches, such as the image's height and width.

```
<img src="images/dog1.gif" height=200 width=150 alt="dog with
                          bone" border=0
```

5. Close the image tag.

```
<img src="images/dog1.gif" height=200 width=150 alt="dog
with bone" border=0>
```

When the browser encounters an image tag, it pulls up and displays the specified image within the HTML page.

TRY THIS:

1. Go to the Try It section (http://www. projectcool.com/guide/html).
2. Type these two paragraphs. Remember to use the paragraph tag. *There are many scenic stops along the way as you drive up the California coast. Be sure to see coastal redwoods. These are in Big Basin in Saratoga, in the Santa Cruz mountains.*
3. Put the cursor in front of the second sentence and add an image. Call the image "trees.gif" (*Hint:* <img src="trees.gif">).
4. Click on TRY IT to see the image within the text.

Using Width and Height Switches

Technically you don't have to specify the exact width and height of your images, but you should. Specifying image width and height lets the browser lay out the page and begin displaying the text while it is still downloading the image. The reader can start using the page immediately instead of waiting for all the images. This increases perceived speed and makes your readers feel as if your site is fast.

Specify image size in pixels. Use your graphics program to see the size of the image in pixels. Save the image file at the exact size you want to use it. Although most browsers will scale the image if the image file and your specified size are different, rescaling consumes computer processing time. Picture the poor reader out there with a 486 PC and 8 megs

perceived speed—The speed at which your readers think your site operates.

of RAM watching the computer go chug-a-chug-a-chug-a as your image rescales on the screen. It is not a pretty sight. And the reader probably won't return.

Using the Image as a Link

One way of attaching an action or additional information to a graphic is to create a hypertext link around it. Chapter 4 covers this process in detail.

One type of item to which people often link from an image is a larger version of the image. Some sites display multiple thumbnails, which are small and require less download time and put in links that readers can click on if they want to see a larger version of the image.

Sometimes people use images as links to other information instead of or in addition to using a text link. For example, a picture of a dog with a bone in a pet site might link to a section on dog nutrition.

Using the Break Tag with an Image

When working with images, you sometimes want the text to follow below the image rather than run alongside the image. The break tag <br> lets you do this. Usually, the break tag stands on its own without any switches. However, the tag does offer one switch: *clear.*

Clear tells the browser to display the content that follows it below the lowest part of the image. By putting a break tag with the clear switch set after a graphic, you ensure that the text that follows the graphic appears underneath the graphic rather than beside it.

The clear switch has three possible values:

▶ *Left* (type *clear=left*) tells the browser to look to the leftmost side of the page and drop the text below the item there.

▶ *Right* (type *clear=right*) tells the browser to look to the rightmost side of the page and drop the text below the item there.

▶ *All* (type *clear=all*) tells the browser to look across the entire page and drop the text below the lowest item on either side.

Figure 5.3 shows the effect of the break tag on an image.

TRY THIS:

1. Go to the Try It section, where you typed the paragraphs: *There are many scenic stops along the way as you drive up the California coast. Be sure to see coastal redwoods. These are in Big*

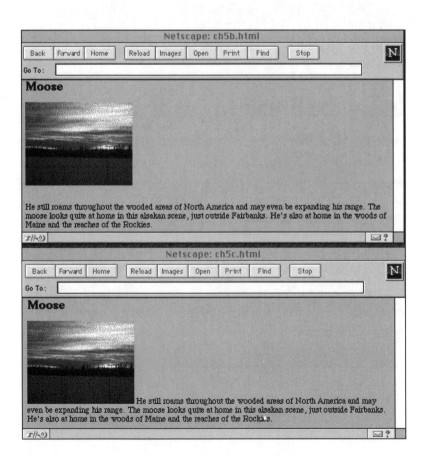

Figure 5.3
*An image with (top)
and without (bottom)
a break tag.*

Basin in Saratoga, in the Santa Cruz mountains.

2. Add a break tag after the image tag.
3. Click on TRY IT to see how the relationship between the text and image changes.

BACKGROUNDS AND COLORS

Inserting an image isn't the only way to use graphics. You can also create a background for your page or add a solid color behind your text. Many people add background images to give their sites identity and personality, as you can see in Figure 5.4. A well-used image or color also makes your page easier on the eyes.

Browsers are set to use their own default colors—typically a gray background, black text, blue links, and purple visited links. Unless you specify otherwise in your HTML file, these are the colors in which your page will display. It is a good idea not only to set your own background image or color, but also to select colors for text, links, and visited links.

You specify backgrounds and colors with the body tag, <body>. You've already learned about the body tag in Chapter 1. The body tag tells the browser that everything

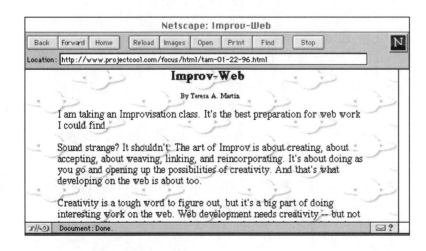

Figure 5.4

A background image can add personality and brand. The small, semitransparent Saturn logo is repeated in the background, like wallpaper. It is subtle and doesn't interfere with the text's readability.

between the start body tag at the beginning of the file and the end-body tag at the end of the file is part of the displayable page. By adding a few switches, you also use the body tag to set text colors and background images or color for the page.

When you use an image as a background, the browser tiles it across the displayable area. It uses your original image and repeats it over and over again. If you are using a pattern, you can create a very small image file to use as your background image. Think of your image as a tiny sample of wallpaper. If you are using a discrete image (for example, we saw a diving page that had a line-art shark as a background) make the image the size you want to see repeated on the page.

> **tiling**—Repeating the same image to fill all available space.

Using the Body Tag

The body tag has five switches:

> ▶ *Background.* Puts the specified image as the background for the page. In the tag, make sure the URL of the image you are using is within quotes.
>
> **TIP:** *If the image resides on your server, use a relative rather than a full link.*

> ▶ *Bgcolor.* Sets a color for the background of the page. Our background color is the hexadecimal representation of off-white. Like the URL, the color name or hex code must be within quotation marks.

> ▶ *Text.* Sets a color for the text. Our text color is the hexadecimal representation of black.

> ▶ *Link.* Sets a color for linked text. Our link color is the hexadecimal representation of gold-brown.

> ▶ *Vlink.* Sets a color for linked text that your reader has already clicked on. Our visited link color is the same as our link color, gold-brown.

To use to body tag:

1. At the beginning of your HTML file, just after the head tags, type the body tag.

   ```
   <body
   ```

2. Type the background switch, followed by the URL of your background image. You don't have to use a background image. If you aren't using an image, just leave out this switch.

   ```
   <body background="pattern1.gif"
   ```

3. Type the background-color switch, followed by the background color you are using.

   ```
   <body background="pattern1.gif" bgcolor="FFFFCC"
   ```

   TIP: *Make sure you set a background color even if you are using a background image. Some people may have images turned off on their browsers; selecting a similar-hued color for a background ensures that all your type will be legible, even if your readers aren't seeing your background image.*

4. Type the text-color switch, followed by the text color you are using.

   ```
   <body background="pattern1.gif" bgcolor="FFFFCC"
   text="000000"
   ```

5. Type the linked-text-color switch, followed by the color in which you want your linked text to appear.

   ```
   <body background="pattern1.gif" bgcolor="FFFFCC"
   text="000000" link="0000FF"
   ```

6. Type the visited-link-text-color switch, followed by the color in which you want to set the links that your readers have already clicked on.

   ```
   <body background="pattern1.gif" bgcolor="FFFFCC"
   text="000000" link="0000FF" vlink="FF00FF"
   ```

   TIP: *Some people like to show readers which links they have already clicked on; others prefer to set their visited link and link colors to be the same. It is a design decision based on the look and feel of your individual site.*

7. End the body tag.

```
<body background="pattern1.gif" bgcolor="FFFFCC"
      text="000000" link="0000FF" vlink="FF00FF">
```

A Few Words about Color

On a Web site, color can be specified in one of two ways:

▶ As a standard computer color name

▶ As a hexadecimal value

On our Web site, at http://www.projectcool.com/ reference/colorchart.html is a chart that shows the standard computer colors by name and how they appear on a monitor. Appendix B also shows a list of color names and their hex values.

There are also a number of programs that let you calculate your hexadecimal color values; some of these are shareware, some are commercial, and there are a number of different ones for each computer platform. If you will be using a lot of color and want to specify it as a hexadecimal, use one of the Web search tools to find a selection of these programs for your platform and test them to see which is most comfortable for you to use.

Here's a few things to think about when you select your colors:

▶ If you are using color, keep in mind that not everyone has the same monitor that you do and that colors look slightly different from computer to computer.

▶ Pick text and background colors that aren't jarring and will hold up for repeat visits. Blood-red on garish green might look dramatic, but how long will you—or your readers—really want to look at it?

▶ Think about readability. On a computer monitor, readability is a major issue. Remember the old green monitors? After staring at them for a while, your eyes would

hexadecimal (hex) value—An alphanumeric code used to represent a specific color.

begin to see the reverse color—pink—when you looked away into space. Text color and background color on a monitor have a strong effect on readability.

TIP: *The human eye is constantly refocusing as it looks at the screen. If you are straining even just a little to read your own page, experiment with different colors. For a while, white type on a reverse background was very popular, but it was difficult to read. We've found than an off-white, subtle yellow, green, or blue background with black type seems to feel comfortable.*

▶ Think about your site's image as you select colors. If possible, coordinate with your overall look and feel. Chartreuse links will feel out of place on site that uses tasteful sketch-style graphics and pastel images.

▶ Use link colors that make sense to your readers and announce the link's presence. We've seen a few sites with links set in the same color as the text. What is the point of a link if no one knows it is there?

A Few Words about Backgrounds

The background switch lets you select an image to use as a background for your page. Like other images, backgrounds can add value—or they can add overhead and make your site unattractive or difficult to read.

Here's a few things to keep in mind as you select your backgrounds:

▶ Make sure the image you select is compatible with the text color you are using. In general, backgrounds should be translucent and simple enough that they don't destroy the legibility of your displayed page. The browser will tile the image so that it repeats itself down and across your display page.

▶ Keep the image file size as small as possible. This helps keep your page slender and quick-loading. Chapter 9 contains a number of tips for minimizing the size of your image file.

▶ If you are using a background image, you still want to specify a background color. Select a background color that is close to the main color of your background image. That way, if readers have the image-loading option of the browser turned off, they will still see a color that is compatible with your type. For example, if you have white type over a dark-purple eggplant image (Ugh! Please don't do this!), you would set your background color as dark purple. Otherwise, a reader who turned off the image-loading option would see white type on a light gray background, making your site unreadable.

Backgrounds and color can add a lot of fun, a lot of design, and a lot of personality to your site. Don't be afraid to experiment with them. One of the nice things about Web publishing is you can play and view your results over and over again before you unleash them on the world.

6

MAKING TABLES

A table presents information in rows and columns. When you think of the word *table,* you probably picture a traditional set of displayed data like a financial table or a set of sports stats.

That's certainly one way to use the HTML table commands. But you can also use the HTML table commands as layout tools, to give the appearance of rows and columns to text and for precise alignment of graphics on a page. Newspaper-style columns and evenly spaced graphics are two common table applications. Tables are also the best way to create forms, the entry blocks of which line up neatly.

As with other HTML tags, the only tool you need to build tables is a text editor. Some of the newer HTML editors, such as Adobe's PageMill 2.0, support tables as well, and if you do a lot of table work you may want to invest in one of these applications. They save you the effort of manually typing every tag within a table.

There really aren't any drawbacks to using tables. Some old, outdated browsers may not support table tags, but all the newer versions do. Don't let historic browsers stop you from using these tags. Remember, although tables can feel tedious to build, they add valuable alignment and formatting capabilities to your page, and they give you the ability to arrange data the way you want it.

> **row**—A set of horizontally displayed information.
>
> **column**—A set of vertically displayed information.

BASIC TABLES

This section introduces HTML table tags. These tags let you display items in table form. The most basic table uses three simple tags and their matching end tags.

`<table>`	Starts a table
`</table>`	Ends a table
`<tr>`	Table row; starts a new row
`</tr>`	Ends a table row
`<td>`	Table data; starts a column with a row
`</td>`	Ends table data

Starting and Ending a Table

You start all tables with the table tag, <table>.

The table tag has five switches:

▶ *Border* lets you set a border around each cell

▶ *Width* lets you set the table width as either a fixed value or as a percentage of the browser window

▶ *Cellspacing* lets you put extra white space between the cells

▶ *Cellpadding* lets you put extra white space inside the cells

▶ *Bgcolor* lets you set a color for the table cells.

For the moment, as you learn to create a basic table, don't worry about any table switches except for *border*.

If you omit the border switch, the table has no borders. If you use the border switch, you can set a border thickness.

For example, if you want a one-unit border, your table tag would look like this:

```
<table border=1>
```

It is a good idea to set a border when you are building a table. That way, you can easily tell the position of your rows and columns and can more easily debug any problems. You can always delete the border switch or set it equal to 0 when your table is perfected.

Always end the table with the end-table tag, </table>. If you omit the end-table tag, the browser won't know where to finish the table and will keep processing it indefinitely. As a result, nothing on the page after the start-table tag will appear in the browser window.

Starting and Ending a Row

A table is made of one or more rows. The very first thing you type after the start-table tag is a table-row tag, <tr>.

The table-row tag has three switches:

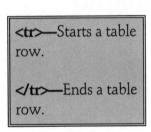

▶ *Align* lets you align the contents of the row horizontally left, right, or center.

▶ *Valign* lets you align the content of the row vertically, to the top, middle, or bottom of the cell.

▶ *Bgcolor* lets you set a color for the cells in this row.

Any values that you set for the row override those that you set for the entire table. For example, if you set a background color of green for a table and then set a background color of blue for the row, the row would be blue. Within each row are several data items. These contain the content of your table. After you've created the content of the row, you end that row with an end-table-row tag, </tr>. Make sure every table-row tag has a corresponding end-table-row tag.

<td>—Starts table data.

</td>—Ends table data.

Starting and Ending a Cell

You create a cell within a row by using a tag called table data, <td>. You end each cell with the end-table-data tag, </td>. Between the start and end tags is the content of the cell.

Each row may have many table-data tags.

The table-data tag has seven switches:

1. *Align* lets you position the contents of the cell aligned left, right, or centered.

2. *Valign* lets you align the content of the cell vertically, to the top, middle, or bottom of the cell.

3. *Bgcolor* lets you set a color for the cell.

4. *Width* lets you enter a width for the cell, either as a fixed size or as a percentage of the table.

5. *Nowrap* tells the browser to display the contents of the cell without autowrapping the contents.

6. *Colspan* tells the browser to let this cell straddle across the specified number of columns.

7. *Rowspan* tells the browser to let this cell straddle across the specified number of rows.

Any values that you set for the individual cell override those that you set for the entire table or row. For example, if you set a background color of blue for the row, and then set a background color of red for the cell, the cell would be red. Figure 6.1 shows a basic table.

Building a Basic Table

To build a basic table:

1. Type *<table* to start the table. Put the table tag on its own line to make it easy to see and find in your ASCII text file.

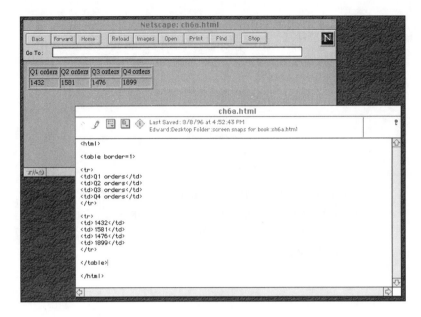

Figure 6.1
A basic table and the tags that built it.

2. Set the table border to 1 or to the value that represents the width you want your table border to be, and end the table tag.

```
<table border=1>
```

TIP: *Remember, it is a good idea to always have a border set when you are building tables. The border makes it easier to find errors and problems in your table, simplifying the debugging process.*

3. Start the first row with a table-row tag.

```
<table border=1>
<tr>
```

4. Type the table-data tag, followed by the first table item.

```
<table border=1>
<tr>
<td>Q1 orders
```

5. At the end of the item, type the end-table-data tag.

```
<table border=1>
<tr>
<td>Q1 orders</td>
```

TIP: *It is a good idea to keep each set of table-data tag/table item/end-table-data tag on the same line.*

6. Type each of the items that you want to appear in the first row. Remember, each item begins and ends with a table-data tag.

```
<table border=1>
<tr>
<td>Q1 orders</td>
<td>Q2 orders</td>
<td>Q3 orders</td>
<td>Q4 orders</td>
```

7. When you have typed all the items in the first row, end the row with the end-row tag. As with the start-table-row tag, it's usually best to put the end-table-row tag on its own line.

```
<table border=1>
<tr>
<td>Q1 orders</td>
<td>Q2 orders</td>
<td>Q3 orders</td>
<td>Q4 orders</td>
</tr>
```

8. Create as many rows as you need in your table. Remember to start and end each with a table-row tag.

9. When the table is complete, end it with the end-table tag.

```
<table border=1>

<tr>
<td>Q1 orders</td>
<td>Q2 orders</td>
<td>Q3 orders</td>
<td>Q4 orders</td>
</tr>

<tr>
<td>1432</td>
<td>1581</td>
<td>1476</td>
<td>1899</td>
</tr>

</table>
```

TIP: *An easy-to-make mistake is to leave off the end-table tag. When this happens, the browser doesn't know what to do, so it just*

stops displaying your page and it looks as if your text has disap-
peared. If you're working with tables and part of your page is "gone,"
double check that the end table tag is present and correct.

TRY THIS:

1. Go to the Try It section (http://www. projectcool.com/guide/html).

2. Start a table with a 1-unit border.

3. Enter these values for the first row:
   East Coast   Midwest   West Coast

4. Enter these values for the second row.
   Atlantic   Great Lakes   Pacific

5. Enter these values for the third row.
   New York   Chicago   Los Angeles

6. End the table and click on TRY IT to see the results.

Adding Rows and Columns

The number of rows and columns in an HTML table expands dynamically. To add an additional column, just add another table data entry, and the browser displays another column.

Adding Text-Formatting Commands

You can include almost every HTML formatting tag you use elsewhere within a table. For example, to set italic text in a cell, just add the italic text tags as you normally would.

```
<tr>
<td><i>Q1 orders</i></td>
```

Adding an Image

The HTML table can contain text and graphics. Adding a graphic is easy. Just type the image command as you normally would. For example, the code to insert an image called Q1.gif would look like this:

```
<tr>
<td><img src="q1.gif" height=50 width=75></td>
```

 TRY THIS: Go to the Try It and edit the table you made earlier:

East Coast	Midwest	West Coast
Atlantic	Great Lakes	Pacific
New York	Chicago	Los Angeles

1. Add the align switch to the first table-row tag to center the header data.

```
<tr align=center>
```

2. Use the bgcolor switch in the table tag to make the cells aqua.

```
<table border=1 bgcolor="aqua">
```

3. Click on TRY IT to see the results.

MORE TABLES

Now that you've mastered the basics of building a table, here are some more tags that let you make your tables richer and more complex.

TIP: *When building a large table, visually organize your tags in your text file. Adding extra empty lines for visual spacing and putting table elements on separate lines makes it much easier to find problems and edit the table in the future.*

Captions

You can add a caption to your table. The caption appears in normal body text, centered, either above or below the table. The caption tag, <caption>, must appear immediately after the table tag and before the first table-row tag. As with all other table tags, you must also use an end-caption tag.

<caption>—Starts a table caption.

</caption>—Ends a table caption.

The caption tag has one switch, *align,* which defines whether the caption appears at the top or bottom of the table.

▶ *Top* (type *align=top*) puts the caption at the top of the table.

▶ *Bottom* (type *align=bottom*) puts the caption at the bottom of the table.

Figure 6.2 shows a table with a caption.

Headers

Headers set at the top of each column in your table. You can manually insert codes to make the headers bold and centered, or you can use the table-header tag to do it for you.

The table-header tag works just like a table-data tag, except it automatically puts the items in bold and centers them.

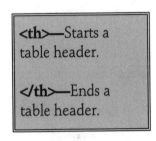

<th>—Starts a table header.

</th>—Ends a table header.

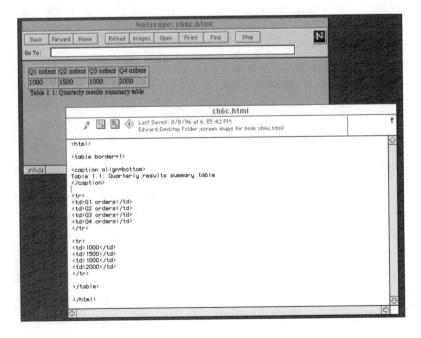

Figure 6.2
A table with a caption.

To make a table header:

1. Start a table header with the table-header tag.

   ```
   <tr>
   <th>
   ```

2. Type your first header.

   ```
   <tr>
   <th>Q1 sales
   ```

3. End the table header.

   ```
   <tr>
   <th>Q1 sales</th>
   ```

4. Repeat for each header you want.

   ```
   <tr>
   <th>Q1 sales</th>
   <th>Q2 sales</th>
   <th>Q3 sales</th>
   <th>Q4 sales</th>
   ```

Spanning Columns

Sometimes you want the data in a cell to span across several columns or even across the whole width of the table. This is called column spanning, and it is controlled by the colspan switch in the table-data tag.

To create a table that looks like the one in Figure 6.3, you'd use the colspan switch.

Spanning Rows

Just as you can have a cell that spans multiple columns, so too can you have a cell that spans multiple rows. Row spanning is controlled with the rowspan switch in the table-data tag.

To create a table that looks like the one in Figure 6.4, you'd use the rowspan switch.

column-spanning cell—A cell that stretches horizontally across several columns.

row-spanning cell—A cell that stretches vertically across several rows.

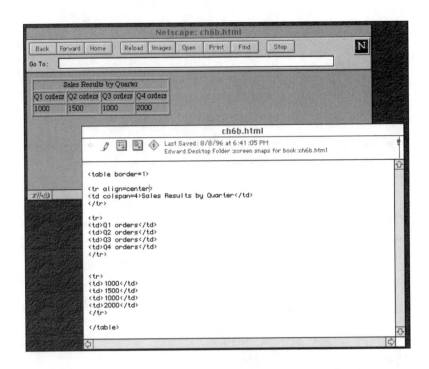

Figure 6.3
A table with a column-spanning cell and the code that created it.

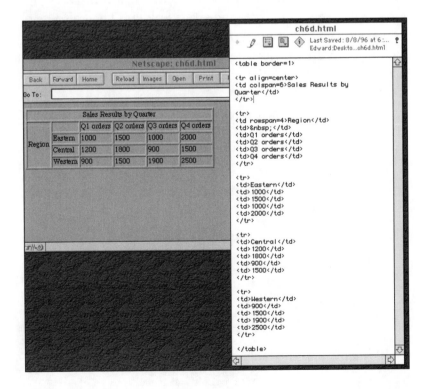

Figure 6.4
A cell with the row-span switch set to four.

When we changed the table to have row-spanning cells, you'll note that we had to change a couple of other things, too.

▶ We had to account for the extra row and change the colspan value in the first row.

▶ We had to add a blank cell as the first cell in the quarter row so that the numbers and the quarter labels would line up correctly.

TIP: *When you change one element in a table, it may have a ripple effect on other parts. It's a good idea to sketch out your table on paper, counting rows and columns where you plan row and column spans. This is also another reason why turning the border on when building the table is a good idea—borders make it easier to see where rows and columns are.*

Using Blank Cells

Blank cells can be very useful when building a complex table. They serve as place- and space holders. They also help you align data when you are using table tags for page layout. Figure 6.4 in the previous section showed an example of using a blank cell for alignment.

 —Non-breaking space.

To create a blank cell:

1. Type the table-data tag.

2. Add the switches to set the size of the cell. The example below sets a cell that is three rows deep and four columns wide.

```
<td rowspan=3 colspan=4>
```

3. Type the nonbreaking-space character. This character is represented by an ampersand, *nbsp,* and a semicolon, with no spaces in between.

```
<td rowspan=3 colspan=4> 
```

4. Finally, end the table-data cell.

```
<td rowspan=3 colspan=4> </td>
```

Using the Align Switches

You can align data in different ways within a cell. The align switch aligns the data horizontally within the cell. The valign switch aligns the data vertically within the cell. Figure 6.5 shows examples of different alignments.

You can use the align and valign switches with the table-header, the table-data, and the table-row tags. If you use these switches with the table-header or table-data tags, the alignment is in effect only for that cell; if you use them with *table row,* the alignment is in effect for all cells in the row.

Preventing a Line Break

Normally, the width of table cells is calculated by the browser. Cell contents will break and wrap as needed. You can, however, override this and tell the browser not to break a line. You control line breaks with the no-wrap switch (*nowrap*) in the table-data tag.

TIP: *Make sure that if you tell the browser not to break a line, the line isn't overly long or you'll end up with an odd, too-wide cell.*

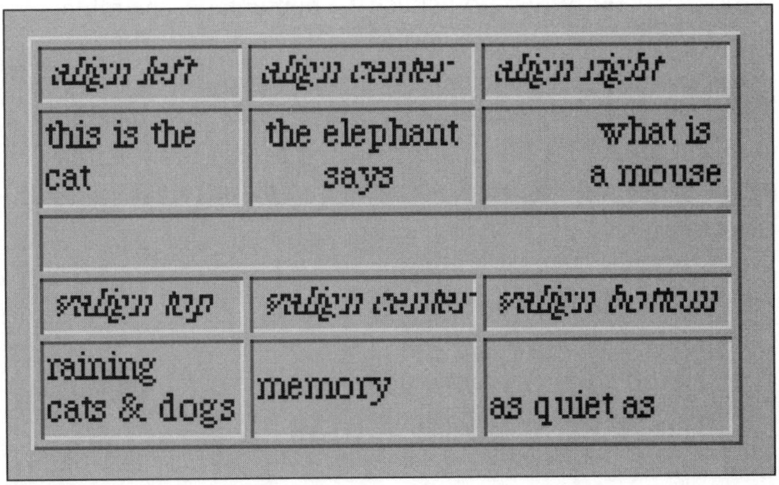

Figure 6.5
The effects of the different alignment switches.

CONTROLLING THE TABLE'S SIZE

Newer browswers, such as Netscape Navigator 2.0/3.0 and Microsoft Internet Explorer (IE) 2.0/3.0, support some additional controls over table and cell size. You can add three switches to the table tag that let you specify spacing in a table, and a new switch in the table-data tag lets you define the width of a cell.

Adjusting Table Width

The width switch lets you specify the width of your table. You can use either a fixed number of units or a percentage of the browser window.

For example, this line sets the table to be 300 units wide:

```
<table border=1 width=300>
```

This line sets the table to be 75 percent of the viewer window:

```
<table border=1 width=75%>
```

If the contents of your table are a certain size, like they would be for a series of graphics, you might want to use a set unit size. Otherwise, you're probably better off using the percentage value. When you specify a set size, the table remains that size no matter how large or small the browser window is, but when you specify a percentage, the table scales with the browser window.

TIP: *No matter how you're specifying table width, each table has a minimum size, and it will never display smaller than that size. The minimum size is the sum of the lengths of all the longest single words in each cell.*

To set a width for your table:

1. Start the table command as you normally would.

```
< table border=3
```

2. Type the width switch and an equals sign.

```
< table border=3 width=
```

3. Type the number of pixels wide you want your table. Or, type the percentage of the screen you want the table to fill, followed by a percent sign. Let us assume that we want the table to fill 75 percent of the screen's width.

```
< table border=3 width=75>
```

4. Continue building your table as you normally would. Column widths are automatically calculated based on the table's width.

Adjusting Cell Width

The width switch in the table-data tag lets you specify the width of a specific cell. You can use either a fixed number of units or a percentage of the browser window.

In general, it is best to let the browser calculate the width automatically, but you can override the browser's setting if you want to achieve a particular effect. For example, the following tag makes the cell fill half the width of the table.

```
<td width=50%>
```

Adjusting Cell Spacing

Cell spacing defines the amount of space between cells in your table. The default value is 2 units; you can change it with the cell-spacing switch, cellspacing, in the table tag. The results appear in Figure 6.6.

```
<table border=1 cellspacing=15>
```

Adjusting Cell Padding

Cell padding defines the amount of space between the edge of the cell and the content of the cell. The default value is

cell spacing—
Space between the outer border of two adjacent cells.

cell padding—
Space between the border of a cell and the data inside it.

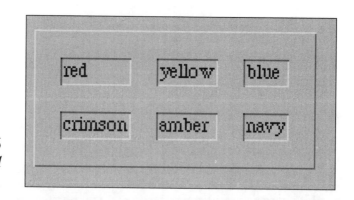

Figure 6.6
A table set with cell spacing of 15 units.

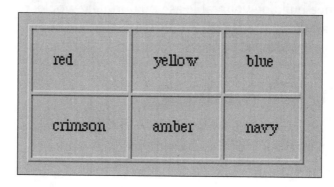

Figure 6.7
A table with a cell padding of 15 units.

1 unit; you can change it with the cell-padding switch, cellpadding, in the table tag. The results are shown in Figure 6.7.

```
<table border=2 cellpadding=15>
```

Cell spacing and padding can be used to your advantage for precise alignment of graphic elements within a table. They can also play an important role in the creation of pseudo-imagemaps, which are discussed in Chapter 7. This amount of control can be important when you are trying to create a particular graphic effect using minumim bandwidth as well.

NESTING TABLES

You can place one table within another. This is called nesting. Nested tables can create some interesting and complex results.

nesting—Placing one table completely within another.

The browser simply treats a nested table as just another piece of content within a cell.

To nest a table within a table:

1. Start the first table as you normally would, defining the table and its rows and cells with the table tags.

2. When you come to the spot where you want to nest the second table, type a table-data tag.

3. Next, type any text you want in the cell with the nested table.

4. Type a comment line, which notes that a nested table is starting. While not necessary to the coding, comment lines make it easier for you to find and edit items later.

5. Type another table tag. This table tag describes the nested table.

6. Build the nested table as you would any other table. Be sure to start and end each row, each table data item, and the table itself.

   TIP: *Don't forget to end the nested table!*

7. At the end of the nested table, type an end-table-data tag. This tag is the matching end tag to the table-data tag you typed before you created the nested table.

8. Finish the first table as you normally would.

Figure 6.8 shows an example of nested tables created by the following code. (It may *look* intimidating, but if you

MAKING TABLES

Figure 6.8
*Four nested tables
within the main table.
Each of the five tables
has its own beginning
and ending tag.*

Sales Results by Quarter												
	Q1 orders			Q2 orders			Q3 orders			Q4 orders		
	Jan.	Feb.	Mar.	Apr.	May.	Jun.	Jul.	Aug.	Sept.	Oct.	Nov.	Dec.
	10%	40%	50%	30%	40%	30%	15%	15%	70%	20%	60%	20%
Eastern	1000			1500			1000			2000		
Central	1200			1800			900			1500		
Western	900			1500			1900			2500		

break it down, it's really just a series of simple table con-
structions.) The nested tables' tags are in bold to highlight
their location:

```
<table border=1>

<tr align=center>
<td colspan=5>Sales Results by Quarter</td>
</tr>

<tr>
<td> </td>
<td>Q1 orders

  <!INSERT NESTED TABLE>
  <table border=1>
  <tr align=center valign=center>
  <td>Jan.</td>
  <td>Feb.</td>
  <td>Mar.</td>
  </tr>

  <tr align=center valign=center>
  <td>10%</td>
  <td>40%</td>
  <td>50%</td>
  </tr>

  </table>

</td>

<td>Q2 orders

  <!INSERT NESTED TABLE>
  <table border=1>
  <tr align=center valign=center>
  <td>Apr.</td>
  <td>May.</td>
```

```
<td>Jun.</td>
</tr>

<tr align=center valign=center>
<td>30%</td>
<td>40%</td>
<td>30%</td>
</tr>

</table>
```

`</td>`

`<td>Q3 orders`

```
<!INSERT NESTED TABLE>
<table border=1>
<tr align=center valign=center>
<td>Jul.</td>
<td>Aug.</td>
<td>Sept.</td>
</tr>

<tr align=center valign=center>
<td>15%</td>
<td>15%</td>
<td>70%</td>
</tr>

</table>
```

`</td>`

`<td>Q4 orders`

```
<!INSERT NESTED TABLE>
<table border=1>
<tr align=center valign=center>
<td>Oct.</td>
<td>Nov.</td>
<td>Dec.</td>
</tr>

<tr align=center valign=center>
<td>20%</td>
<td>60%</td>
<td>20%</td>
</tr>

</table>
```

```
</td>
</tr>

<tr>
<td>Eastern</td>
<td>1000</td>
<td>1500</td>
<td>1000</td>
<td>2000</td>
</tr>

<tr>
<td>Central</td>
<td>1200</td>
<td>1800</td>
<td>900</td>
<td>1500</td>
</tr>

<tr>
<td>Western</td>
<td>900</td>
<td>1500</td>
<td>1900</td>
<td>2500</td>
</tr>

</table>
```

COOL USES FOR TABLES

As we noted at the beginning of this chapter, table tags can be applied to create different page-layout effects. Here's a few to give you some starting ideas.

Tables for Page Layout

Tables can be an effective tool in HTML page layout. Careful use of them allows you precise control over how your page will appear to the end user. This can be especially important with graphics that need to be precisely placed or elements that need to retain their relative visual relationship.

Figures 6.9–6.12 show examples of a table used to position page elements. The code that created each page follows the illustration.

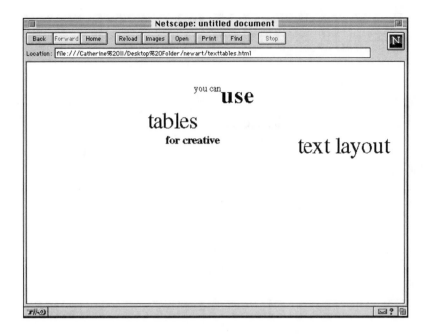

Figure 6.9
Figure 6.9
Text arranged on the page.

In the first, we wanted text arranged on the page in a specific layout, as shown in Figure 6.9.

One approach to creating this page would be to create the entire image in Photoshop or in a layout program, save it as a GIF and insert the entire GIF. However, with tables you can create the same effect—and use significantly less bandwidth—by using HTML text and the font tag.

Figure 6.10 shows the underlying table for this layout. The table uses two rows and three columns. The table is a fixed width, as we wanted to keep the relative relationship between the cell items if the browser window were to be resized.

Notice that we create the table with borders turned on. Once the layout is to our satisfaction, we turn the borders off and the table is invisible. The reader sees a nicely arranged page and never once thinks of it as a table.

We use nonbreaking space bands to hold blank columns and the font tag to vary the size of the text.

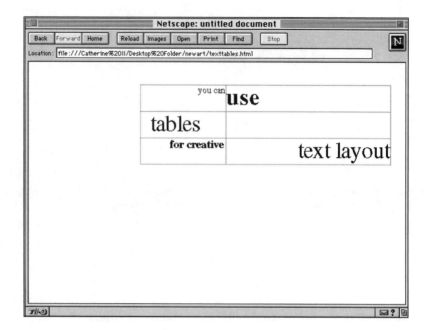

Figure 6.10
With borders turned on, you can see the underlying table.

The following is the HTML code for this page.

```
<table width="400" border="1" cellspacing="0" cellpadding="0">
<tr>
<td colspan="2" valign="top" align="right" width="0%"><font
size=+1>you
can</font></td>
<td width="90" valign="bottom"><b><font
size=+4>use</font></b></td></tr>
<tr>
<td colspan="2">  <font size=+4> tables</font></td>
<td> </td></tr>
<tr>
<td colspan="2" valign="top" align="right"> <b><font
size=+2>for
creative</font></b> </td>
<td align="right" valign="top"><font size=+4>text
layout</font></td></tr>
</table>
```

TIP: *If you wanted to use real type instead of HTML text, you could create the effect by positioning several small GIFs, each holding one word. The net result is still smaller and faster than one large GIF and also easier to update or change if you needed to edit it.*

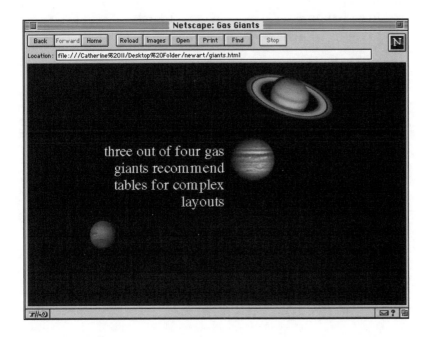

Back Forward Home   Reload Images Open Print Find   Stop

Location: file:///Catherine%20II/Desktop%20Folder/newart/giants.html

three out of four gas
giants recommend
tables for complex
layouts

Figure 6.11
It looks like an illus-
tration with overlaid
text.

In the second, we wanted to create a layout combing text and images of planets, as shown in Figure 6.11.

Again, we could have created on large GIF, but it would have been a large file for readers to download.

Instead, we built a table, used padding and spacing for accurate positioning, and placed three small GIFs with HTML text.

Figure 6.12 shows the underlying table.

The following is the code that created the table. You'll note that we follow the usual rules for using graphics, including specifying each graphic's width and height.

```
<table width="400" border="0" cellspacing="2" cellpadding="0">
<tr>
<td width="197" height="99"> </td>
<td width="42%" valign="top" align="right"> <img
src="images/saturn1.jpg" width="150" height="83"></td>
</tr>
<tr>
```

```
<td width="197" valign="top"><table border="0" cellspacing="2"
cellpadding="0" width="100%" height="129">
<tr>
<td><div align=right><p><font size=+3>three out of four gas giants
recommend
tables for complex layouts</font></div></td>
</tr>
</table>
<img src="images/neptune.jpg" width="50" height="50"></td>
<td width="197" valign="top"> <img src="images/jupiter.jpg"
width="75" height="75" align="bottom"></td>
</tr>
</table>
```

In both cases, the tables are invisible to the reader. The result doesn't look like a traditional row and column layout. Yet the table commands added formatting power to the HTML page and created a neat and effective result.

The moral of this chapter? Be creative in using tables; don't relegate them only to financial statements or rows of numbers. It's amazing how much formatting power they can bring to your Web site.

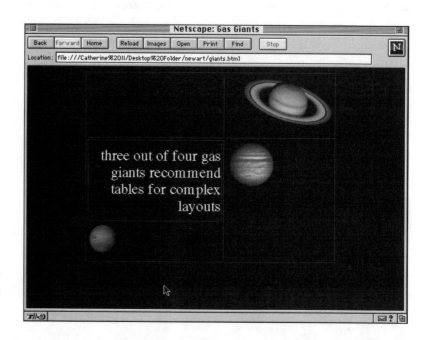

Figure 6.12
The illustration is really several small illustrations arranged in a table.

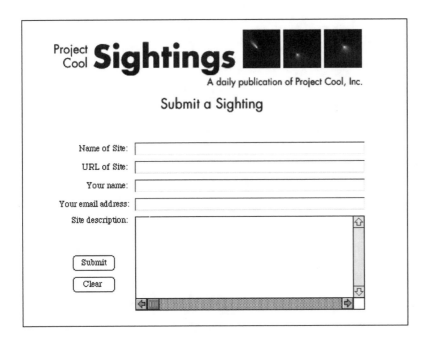

Figure 6.13
Form layout created using tables with borders turned off.

Tables for Form Alignment

One of the biggest problems with forms on the Web is that they are ugly due to lack of any alignment. You can fix this by placing your forms in a table and carefully using the table-alignment commands. Take a look at the form in Figure 6.13.

Notice how the text is aligned right against the text-entry fields. Also note how the buttons are nontraditionally placed. All this is done with the table-alignment features. We'll be discussing exactly how this is accomplished in our chapter on forms.

As you can see, tables are a useful tool for many aspects of Web-site design. Hand-coding complex tables is detailed work, but the results can be quite powerful and useful. If you're turned off by the amount of work in creating complex tables, check out the newer HTML layout packages, but don't give up on the table features. They can add a lot to your site.

7
IMAGEMAPS

Imagemaps let you place a picture on a Web page and use parts of the picture as navigational aids. Imagemaps are a tool for making your page more visual and making information easier to present and understand. The classic application of the imagemap is a literal map of a geographical area, with links to regional information embedded in the map graphic. Figure 7.1 illustrates an imagemap.

> **imagemap—**
> A graphic with embedded, invisible links.

There are currently three types of imagemap technology:

- ▶ Server-side
- ▶ Client-side
- ▶ Pseudo

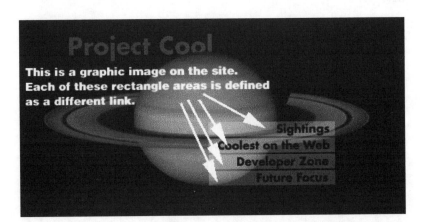

Figure 7.1
An imagemap with four defined and linked areas.

server-side—
An imagemap in which the program that maps the links to the image lives on the server.

client-side—
An imagemap in which the browser interprets the image link information, all of which is contained within the HTML file.

pseudo-imagemap—An imagemap in which common HTML techniques mimic the effect of an actual image-map without any special imagemap programs.

Each imagemap, regardless of its type, displays two kinds of information. One is the graphic image. The other is an embedded set of links.

A server-side imagemap is one in which the link information is contained at the server using a custom map information file. Server-side imagemaps require a browser capable of displaying graphics and a server with an imagemap program.

A client-side imagemap contains all necessary information within the HTML page itself. Not all browsers support client-side imagemaps.

A pseudo-imagemap is a technology that looks and acts like an imagemap through careful use of HTML tags but offers some bandwidth flexibility and doesn't rely on a server or special browser. It will even work on text-only browsers such as Lynx.

SELECTING IMAGES

When you add an imagemap, you are adding overhead to your Web site. It will take your readers extra time to download the imagemap. So you'd better be sure what you're creating is worth the extra effort.

Here's some things to think about when adding an imagemap:

▶ Select an image that adds meaning to the information. Ask yourself: Would the site be just as easy or logical to use if the image weren't here? If the answer is yes, think carefully about why you are using an imagemap.

▶ Select an image that makes sense as an imagemap. Will the image leave your readers wondering: What do I do next? Will it be clear where to click on the image and what clicking in the different places will do? As you do elsewhere in Web design, it is better to err on the side of the clear and obvious than on the side of the cute and clever. Remember, we're talking bandwidth here. You want to entice readers to stay and use your site.

▶ Select an image that is well executed. A sloppy, poorly created graphic doesn't add value to your site and can turn away your readers.

▶ Select an image that has some relevance to your site's look and feel. The imagemap is an integral part of your Web site's design and user interface, not a way to prove that you know about imagemap technology.

DECIDING UPON LINKS

Once you've selected an image, you'll need to decide where you want the links within the image. For all types of image-maps, this means deciding what portions of the image should link to which URL. For server- and client-side image-maps it also means finding the *x* and *y* coordinates of those portions. For the pseudo-imagemap, you need to think about logical ways to divide up the image, ideally into horizontal slices, so that each piece has its own link.

The best way to find the coordinates is though the image-creation program you are using. For example, the Photoshop Info Palette displays the *x* and *y* coordinates in the bottom box of the palette as you move your cursor over the image (see Figure 7.2).

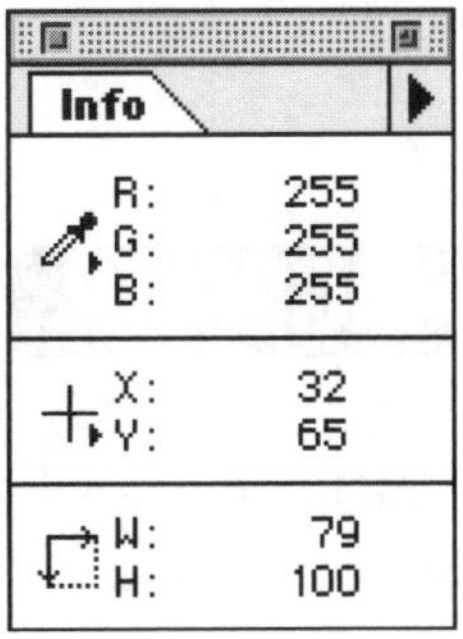

***x,y* coordinates—** The horizontal (*x*) and vertical (*y*) pixel location of a link.

Figure 7.2
Your graphic program can show you the x *and* y *coordinates.*

TIP: *It is a good idea to sketch out, on paper, your image and its links and think about how it will work before you sit down to create the imagemap.*

Here are a few things to think about as you decide how to divide and link the image:

▶ Will the links make logical sense to your readers? Will it be clear that they can click on the portion? Will they understand what happens when they click on each section?

▶ What shape will the links be? You can create rectangles, circles, and polygons. You'll need to know the upper left and lower right coordinates for rectangles, the location of the center point and one point on a circle's circumference, and the coordinates for each angle on a polygon.

▶ Will every spot on the imagemap link to a specific URL? What happens when your readers click on an in-between space? (You can select a default link that gets activated when readers click in a spot that you haven't otherwise defined.)

▶ What happens if your readers are using a text-only browser, like Lynx, or have turned off graphics in their browser?

A little preparation and forethought helps your imagemaps add value to your site and be truly useful to your readers.

CREATING A SERVER-SIDE IMAGEMAP

A server-side imagemap is an imagemap in which the browser sends the server the coordinates of the imagemap. The server then translates the coordinates into a URL and returns the URL to the browser.

There are two steps to creating a server-side imagemap:

1. Create a map file. This file defines each link and its coordinates within the graphic.

2. Create an HTML file that calls the imagemap.

To use a server-side imagemap, the server that hosts your Web site must have an imagemap program running. Typically, this program is located in the cgi-bin directory. It is usually called *imagemap*. Check with your ISP to be sure that the server hosting your site can handle server-side imagemaps.

> **map file**—The file that contains the link coordinates and URLs for an imagemap.

Building the Map File

The map file defines the location and link for each clickable area on the image. It is a simple, ASCII text file that describes the *x* (horizontal) and *y* (vertical) pixel coordinates of the links. Every imagemap must have a corresponding map file.

Map filenames must always end with the extension .map. Without this extension, the browser won't be able to identify the map file as such.

You need no special tools for creating a map file other than a text editor. However, it is helpful to have your graphics-creation program running and the original graphic on your screen as you create the map file. Look at the appropriate tool within your graphics program to see the *x* and *y* pixel coordinates of the image as you create links for it.

Each line in the file defines one link on the imagemap. For example, this is the map file for our Contents page:

```
default http://www.projectcool.com
rect http://www.projectcool.com/sightings 141,114 372,143
rect http://ww.projectcool.com/coolest 141,154 372,183
rect http://www.projectcool.com/developer 141,194 372,223
rect http://www.projectcool.com/focus 141,234 372,263
```

Note that:

- ▶ The file is straight text, not HTML tags.

- ▶ Each item in the line is separated with a space.

- ▶ The first line in the map file is the default action. This is what happens if the reader clicks in an undefined area of the imagemap. In this case, the default action is, "Go to the URL www.projectcool.com."

- ▶ Each succeeding line in the file defines a link on the graphic. On our contents page, we defined four links, each one a button that takes the reader to a different URL.

As we mentioned previously, you can make links in one of three shapes:

- ▶ Rectangle

- ▶ Circle

- ▶ Polygon

To define a rectangular link, as shown in Figure 7.3:

- ▶ Type *rect.* This says that the shape is to be a rectangle.

- ▶ Type the URL to which this shape is linked.

- ▶ Type the pixel coordinates for the upper left corner of the rectangle.

- ▶ Type the pixel coordinates for the lower right corner of the rectangle.

To define a circular link, as shown in Figure 7.4:

- ▶ Type *circle.* This says that the shape is to be a circle.

- ▶ Type the URL to which this shape is linked.

- ▶ Type the pixel coordinates for the centerpoint of the circle.

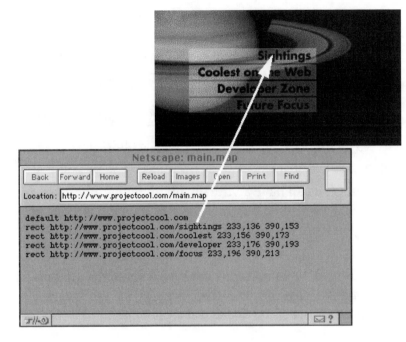

Figure 7.3
A rectangular link.

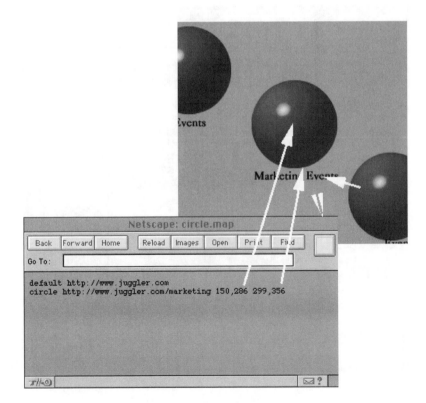

Figure 7.4
A circular link.

- Type the pixel coordinates for any one point on the circle's circumference.

To define a polygon link, as shown in Figure 7.5:

- Type *poly*. This says that the shape is to be a polygon.

- Type the URL to which this shape is linked.

- Type the pixel coordinates for each corner of the polygon. You can have a virtually unlimited number of corners. Make sure you enter them in sequential order, as if you were connecting the dots.

TIP: *You don't have to close the polygon by reentering the beginning coordinates. The polygon automatically closes itself with a straight line between the last set of coordinates and the first one.*

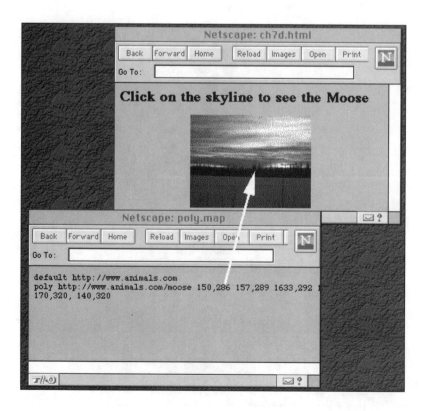

Figure 7.5
A polygon link.

To build the map file:

1. Create a file, the name of which ends with the extension .map.

2. In the file, type *default.* Then press the space bar and enter the URL for default link for the image. This is the page that gets displayed if the reader clicks on an undefined area of the image. Typically, the default is the page in which the imagemap appears.

3. Create each link. Remember, the basic format for links is:

```
linktype (space) URL for linked page (space) x,y coordinates
```

4. Save and close the file.

Placing an Imagemap in an HTML File

The final step in using an imagemap is building the actual HTML page that incorporates the imagemap.

TIP: *Before you put an imagemap onto an HTML page, you must have created a map file for that image.*

Now that you've built the map file, you're ready to use your imagemap. This is the HTML file that calls the imagemap for our Contents page. The parts that call the imagemap are in bold.

```
<html>
<head>
<title>Project Cool: Main</title>
</head>
<body bgcolor="000000" text="cccccc" link="d2691e"
vlink="d2691e">
<p align=center>
<a href="/cgi-bin/imagemap/main.map"><img
src="images/venusmenu.gif" width=411 height=399 border=0
alt="" ISMAP></a>
<p align=center>
<font size=+1>
```

```
| <a href="sightings">Sightings</a> |
<a href="coolest">Coolest on the Web</a>
| <a href="developer">Developer Zone</a> |
<a href="focus">Future Focus</a> |

</body>
</html>
```

To use an imagemap in an HTML file:

1. Place the cursor at the spot in the file where you want the imagemap to appear. Enter an anchor-reference tag that identifies the name and location of the imagemap program on the server, and the name of the map file. For example, we use this reference tag:

   ```
   <a href="/cgi-bin/imagemap/main.map">
   ```

   On our server, the imagemap program is in the cgi-bin directory, the imagemap program is called "imagemap," and the map file we are using is named "main.map."

   TIP: *With server-side imagemaps, there are subtle differences between different servers. The code above works with NCSA and most other servers, except Netscape. Netscape doesn't require the path to the imagemap program or the name of the program, as these are already incorporated into the Netscape server. If your pages are hosted on a Netscape server, the first line would simply read <a href="main.map">.*

2. Enter an image tag that identifies the image onto which you are mapping the links. The final item in the image tag is the command ismap, which tells the browser that this image is actually an imagemap. For example:

   ```
   <img src="images/venusmenu.gif" width=411 height=399
   border=0 alt="" ISMAP>
   ```

   This tells the browser to display the GIF file "images/venusmenu.gif." It uses the optional width, depth, border, and alt calls, just as you would when using a plain image. Finally, it uses the ismap call to tell the browser this image is really a server-side imagemap and should go to the server for processing.

---

ismap—A switch that goes in the tag <img> and tells the browser that the image is also an imagemap.

3. Enter tags to create hyperlinked text, which duplicates the links in the imagemap. This ensures that everyone, whether they use graphics or not, can see the link options.

CREATING A CLIENT-SIDE IMAGEMAP

Now that you understand server-side imagemaps, client-side mapping will be a breeze. Client-side imagemaps are like server-side maps except that the map definition is contained within the HTML of the Web page. They also put no extra demand on the server, so they execute faster than server-side maps. Most newer browsers support the client-side map tags.

Here is what the same map used in our server-side example looks like as a client-side map:

```
<map name="mainmap">
<area shape="rect" coords="141,114,372,143" href="/sightings">
<area shape="rect" coords="141,154,372,183" href="/coolest">
<area shape="rect" coords="141,194,372,223" href="/developer">
<area shape="rect" coords="141,234,372,263" href="/focus">
<area shape="rect" coords="0,0,460,266" nohref>
</map>
```

Instead of being a separate file, the map data has become an HTML tag, somewhat like a table tag. It starts with a map tag. In between are a number of area tags that define each clickable link in the image. It ends with </map>.

All the same shapes that were used in the server-side map file still apply. The one difference is that the default link is the last area tag within the map definition. It specifies that the entire area of the image, from upper left to lower right, has no href link, so that clicking on any spot on the image that is not within one of the other area definitions will produce no results.

Map Tags

There are three map tags.

The first, <map>, starts a map definition. It has one switch, name. The name you are giving this map definition must be surrounded by quotation marks, like this: *<map name="myhomepage">*.

The second, <area>, defines each clickable area on the image and its link. You may have many area tags within a map definition. *Area* has three switches:

▶ *Shape.* Defines the shape of the linked area. The possible values are *rect, circle, poly,* and *point. Point* is an individual point on the image.

▶ *Coords.* Sets the coordinates of the area. Remember, for a rectangle, you set the upper left and lower right coordinates. For a circle, you set the centerpoint and a point on the circumference. On a polygon, you specify every angle. On a point, you specify a single set of coordinates.

▶ *href.* Sets the link for the specified area. It can be either a full or a relative URL.

Applying the Map to an Image

To use the map with a specific image requires that you add a switch to the image tag that calls the image in the HTML file. This new switch is *usemap*. The value of *usemap* is a pound sign (#) followed by the name you gave the map definition, like this:

```
<img src="images/mainmap.jpg" width=460 height=266 USEMAP="#mainmap">
```

You can still use this type of mapping in conjunction with server-side mapping for those users who might have older browsers that don't support client-side mapping. Simply use the server-side mapping around the client-side image tag including the ISMAP switch like this:

```
<href="/cgi-bin/imagemap/main.map">
<img src="images/mainmap.jpg" width=460 height=266 USEMAP="#mainmap" ISMAP>
</a>
```

CREATING A PSEUDO-IMAGEMAP

A pseudo-imagemap is really a series of images butted up against one another so that seams are invisible. To create one, you build a large image and chop it into logical sections. Using HTML and placing the images against one another creates the effect of one single image, but sections of it can be links as needed. Individual sections are also replaceable from page to page.

Pseudo-imagemaps are a very powerful way of implementing an imagemap with much greater flexibility than either the server- or client-side technology. You might want to consider the pseudo-imagemap if bandwidth is a major consideration or if your readers might have browsers that don't support graphics or client-side imagemaps.

TIP: *The pseudo-imagemap technique lends itself to many applications that don't require clickable links. For example, they can be used to replace one portion of an image, such as the numbers in a scoreboard.*

Creating the Pseudo-Imagemap Graphic

The first thing you need to create for a pseudo-imagemap is the graphic image you want your readers to see.

When creating this graphic, consider how it will need to be sliced up. Each of the chunks will probably be a link to someplace else within your site.

Ideally, your graphic should be easily divisible into rectangular slices. If you can divide it into several horizontal sections, it will require less work on your part than if you must break it into multiple sections, both horizontal and vertical. If your graphic must be divided into vertical and horizontal chunks, you'll use table commands to reassemble it in proper order.

Let's take a look at how one of our current pages at Project Cool is put together as a pseudo-imagemap. Figure 7.6 shows the page.

This page was created entirely as a graphic in Photoshop, then cut into discrete pieces and reassembled within a table in HTML. Figure 7.7 shows what the individual pieces look like.

This page is a table that has three rows. The second row is divided into two columns, and the second column contains four discrete graphics. We've added dividing lines

Figure 7.6
A sample page from the Project Cool Web site that was created using a pseudo-imagemap.

Figure 7.7
The pieces into which the original graphic was divided.

between those four graphics so that you see how they are cut up, but in reality there is no space between them.

Creating Pseudo-Imagemap Links

Now that there's an image, the next step is to add links to each piece of the image. Let's look at the source code that makes this page work.

```
<html>
<head>
<title>Project Cool Sighting 07/16/96</title>
</head>
<body bgcolor="ffffff" text="cccccc" link="0083bf" vlink="0083bf">
<div align=center>
<table cellpadding=0 cellspacing=0 border=0>
<tr>
<td colspan=2>
<img src="images/sightingslogo.gif" width=450 height=82 alt="Project Cool
Sightings">
</td>
</tr>
<tr>
```

```
<td>
<img src="images/describe.gif" width=247 height=96 alt="">
</td>
<td>
<a href="http://www.projectcool.com"><img src="images/today.gif"
width=200 height=30 border=0 alt="Today's sighting"></a><br><a
href="previous.html"><img src="images/previous.gif"
width=200 height=18 border=0 alt="Previous sightings"></a><br><a
href="submit.html"><img src="images/submit.gif"
width=200 height=18 border=0 alt="Submit a sighting"></a><br><a
href="/"><img src="images/return.gif"
width=200 height=30 border=0 alt="Return to Project Cool"></a>
</td>
</tr>
<tr>
<td colspan=2>
<img src="images/copyright.gif" width=450 height=70 alt="Copyright 1996
Project Cool, Inc.">
</td>
</tr>
</table>
</div>
</body>
</html>
```

Starting from the top, we have our standard HTML header information. The first place that we start building the image is with our table command.

```
<table cellpadding=0 cellspacing=0 border=0>
```

We've set cell padding and cell spacing to zero so that we can minimize the space between images. We've also turned off that ugly table border. Frankly, we've never found a good use for the default-style table borders, and they have absolutely no place in an imagemap, where we want to maintain the continuity of the image.

When you look at the code, you see what basically amounts to a table. The one place that it is different is in the following section, describing the clickable buttons that go to different pages.

```
<td>
<a href="http://www.projectcool.com"><img src="images/today.gif"
width=200 height=30 border=0 alt="Today's sighting"></a><br><a
```

```
href="previous.html"><img src="images/previous.gif"
width=200 height=18 border=0 alt="Previous sightings"></a><br><a
href="submit.html"><img src="images/submit.gif"
width=200 height=18 border=0 alt="Submit a sighting"></a><br><a
href="/"><img src="images/return.gif"
width=200 height=30 border=0 alt="Return to Project Cool"></a>
</td>
```

This is how we create a seamless map in one of the cells. When you first look at the source code, you might think it is a bit confusing. Well, that's because in order to make this effect work fully, you need to eliminate anything that a Web browser might interpret as an empty-space character. That includes carriage returns outside of HTML tags. If there is anything extra outside a tag, a browser will interpret it as a space and insert a space between graphics—and you'll end up with a graphic that has seams.

Close examination of the code reveals that there is no line break that is not within an HTML tag. This allows us to make the graphics touch and minimize space. This allows us to have a seemingly seamless graphic that works even if you have a different background color set.

Another important thing to note is that all link borders are set to zero so that we don't have anything added by the browser. After all, if we want a seamless graphic, we certainly don't want extra boxes drawn inside it. Also notice that all graphics have alt settings, specifying alternate text. This allows these map types to work with text-only Web browsers and for modem users who might keep images turned off to save download time.

With those simple techniques, you can build nearly anything. Now that you've learned the secret of pseudo-imagemaps, go forth and divide.

Other Pseudo-Imagemap Applications

One application for pseudo-imagemaps is to use them to change a single part of a larger graphic. This saves bandwidth and lets you create some interesting effects. Figures

7.8–7.12 show how to create two different effects using pseudo-imagemaps in this way.

The ideas are really endless—you can apply the pseudo-imagemap technique to any large graphic that has one small, updatable part. These are just a few ideas to get you started. You can see the real working versions of these two examples at the Try It Web site, http://www.projectcool.com/guide/html.

Figure 7.8 shows a graphical scoreboard. Only the score sections change, requiring minimal download time to update.

This is the code that created the scoreboard. Figure 7.9 illustrates the individual pieces that make up the full scoreboard. You'll note that there are no line breaks or extra spaces between tags. Any line breaks must occur in the middle of a tag to prevent extra white spaces in your pseudo-imagemap.

```
<body bgcolor=ffffff>
<div align=center>
<img src="images/tsports.gif" width=300 height=30 alt="Theatre
Sports"><br
><img src="images/spacer.gif" width=15 height=40 alt=" "><img
src="images/0.gif"
width=45 height=40 alt="0"><img src="images/7.gif"
width=45 height=40 alt="7"><img src="images/finals.gif" width=90
height=40
alt=" to "><img src="images/1.gif"
width=45 height=40 alt="1"><img src="images/3.gif"
width=45 height=40 alt="3"><img src="images/spacer.gif"
width=15 height=40 alt=""><br><img src="images/teams.gif"
width=300 height=30 alt="Black Ties vs Gatecrashers">
</div>
</body>
```

Figure 7.10 shows a button menu. Only one button changes to reflect the reader's choice. It tells the reader what option he or she has selected or where he or she is located within the site without requiring the time to download the entire menu graphic.

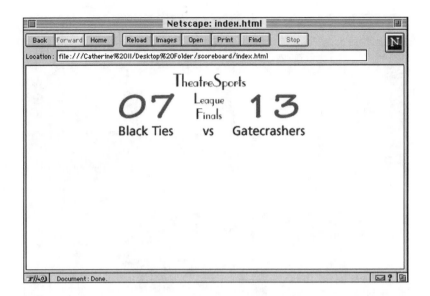

Figure 7.8
This graphic scoreboard can update in near-real time by downloading the small graphic files that contain the numbers.

In this example, when a reader clicks on a button, the visual effect displays a pushed-in button and the message "Great Choice!" appears. Figure 7.11 shows how the screen looks after the reader makes a choice. Clicking on the same button again clears the choice.

The visual feedback could be anything, though. For example, we could have made the selected flavor appear in red type with a gold halo if we'd wanted. The technique is the same regardless of the specific images being replaced.

This is the code that created the flavor list the reader sees when he or she first enters the site. The file is named "flavors.html." Again, notice that there are no line breaks or

Figure 7.9
This illustration shows the individual pieces of graphic that combine together to build one larger graphic. Note that the score graphics are small and can be quickly and easily updated, giving the appearance of a real-time scoreboard.

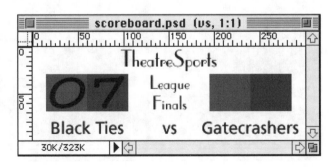

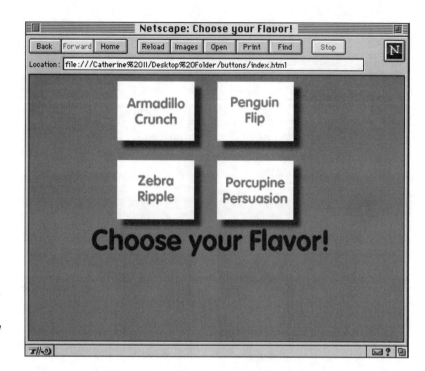

Figure 7.10
The visual button choices offered to a reader.

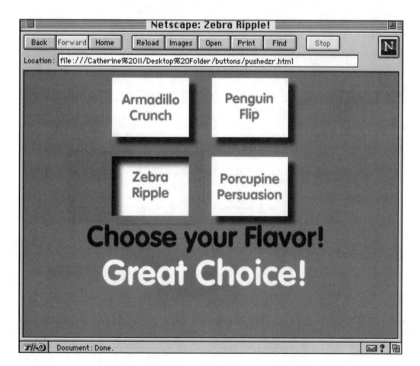

Figure 7.11
This screen shows the flavor the reader selected and congratulates him or her on the choice. The pseudo-imagemap allows graphical feedback without the need to download a complete graphic.

extra spaces between tags. Any line breaks must occur in the middle of a tag to prevent extra white spaces in your pseudo-imagemap. Pay particular attention to the areas that call the graphic "zr.gif." You'll see that there is an <a href> link on the graphic that calls a file named "pushedzr.html."

```html
<html>
<head>
<title>Choose your Flavor!</title>
</head>
<body bgcolor="9c9c9c">
<div align=center>
<a href="pushedac.html"><img src="images/ac.gif" width=179
height=92
border=0 alt="Armadillo Crunch"></a><a href="pushedpf.html"
><img src="images/pf.gif" width=179 height=92 border=0
alt="Penguin Flip"></a><br><a href="pushedzr.html"
><img src="images/zr.gif" width=179 height=92 border=0
alt="Zebra Ripple"></a><a href="pushedpp.html"
><img src="images/pp.gif" width=179 height=92 border=0
alt="Porcupine Persuasion"></a><br
><img src="images/choose.gif" width=358 height=41
alt="Choose your Flavor!">
</div>
</body>
</html>
```

When a reader selects Zebra Ripple, a new HTML page named "pushedzr.html" is called. The page uses almost all the same graphics. The cached graphics are reused, and the two small new elements fall into place. Additionally, the name in the title bar changes to "Zebra Ripple!" This is the code for the second HTML page.

Again, pay particular attention to the image named "pushedzr.gif." You'll see that it links to an HTML file named "flavors.html." This creates a toggle effect. Click on the button, and it appears pushed in. Click on it again, and it appears popped out and the "great choice" message disappears.

```html
<html>
<head>
<title>Zebra Ripple!</title>
</head>
```

```
<body bgcolor="9c9c9c">
<div align=center>
<a href="pushedac.html"><img src="images/ac.gif" width=179
height=92
border=0 alt="Armadillo Crunch"></a><a href="pushedpf.html"
><img src="images/pf.gif" width=179 height=92 border=0
alt="Penguin Flip"></a><br><a href="flavors.html"
><img src="images/pushedzr.gif" width=179 height=92 border=0
alt="Zebra Ripple"></a><a href="pushedpp.html"
><img src="images/pp.gif" width=179 height=92 border=0
alt="Porcupine Persuasion"></a><br
><img src="images/choose.gif" width=358 height=41
alt="Choose your Flavor!"><br
><img src="images/choice.gif" width=358 height=44 alt="Great
Choice!">
</div>
</body>
</html>
```

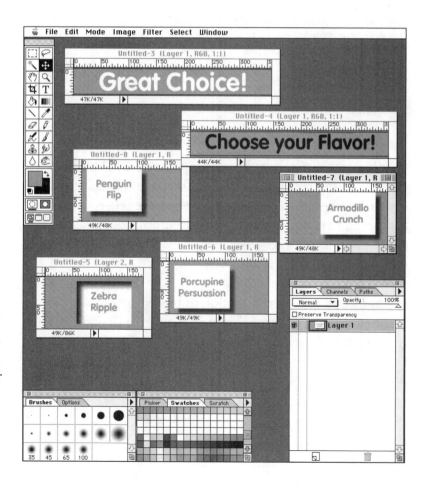

Figure 7.12
This illustration shows the individual graphic pieces that make up the larger image. Any one of these pieces can be quickly and easily pulled into an HTML page.

This effect requires no special server software and no special browser support. It gives you a nice sense of motion, using minimal bandwidth with simple HTML code.

Figure 7.12 illustrates the individual pieces that make up the buttons. Each of these is an individual graphic, pulled together using pseudo-imagemap techniques.

Here's a few other ideas you might want to explore on your own.

▶ Use a pseudo-imagemap to remove a book from a bookshelf.

▶ Use a pseudo-imagemap to light up a traffic signal.

▶ Use a pseudo-imagemap to update the daily special on a fixed luncheon menu.

Remember, pseudo-imagemaps are a great, low-bandwidth way to update a graphic. Their use is limited only by your imagination.

DESIGNING WITH FRAMES

Frames are a way of dividing an HTML page into different sections, each displaying different content. With frames you can continually display components, such as navigational buttons, in the browser. You can also define the relationship between pieces of the Web page. Figure 8.1 shows how we used frames to keep a consistent table of contents in our Coolest page. When a reader clicks on an item in the table of contents, the selected section appears in the large frame to the right. The table of contents remains fixed on the screen as a navigational bar.

The frame tag set was introduced by Netscape in Navigator 2.0 and appears in the current version of NCSA Mosaic and Microsoft Internet Explorer. Some people say that frames aren't part of the standard and advocate avoiding them, but if you use them well and your audience has recent browsers, they can be a powerful addition to your site.

PLANNING FOR FRAMES

Well-applied frames make complex information easier to navigate. They let you create paths, help you show people where they are and where they can go next, and provide some often needed structure. They're a little like grids in the print design world in that they define the underlying struc-

> **grid**—The underlying structure of a design.

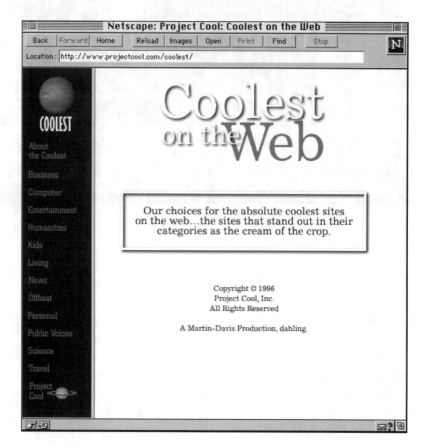

Figure 8.1
The Coolest on the Web page, which was designed to take advantage of the frame features.

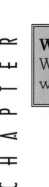
ture within which information will be displayed. You can limit your communication to one basic, wide, undefined column, or you can create a framework that quietly adds complexity and interest without adding confusion.

> **WYSIWYG—** What you see is what you get.

The frame tags themselves are easy to learn and use, and emerging WYSIWYG HTML editors make the mechanics of frames even easier. But with frames, the trick isn't in the tool—it's in the application. Frames are a good tool . . . if they're used well.

What you need to remember is that, when you work with frames, you are essentially creating a user interface for your Web site. Most people who haven't done a good job with frames haven't thought through their site design.

Normally, when you change pages in your browser, the entire page repaints. But, by using frames, you can change the content of one portion of the page while leaving the content of another untouched. Additionally, a click you make in one frame can control what appears in another. All of this makes frames an ideal way of handling items like tables of contents. You can look at your options and your current choice simultaneously.

Here's a few questions to ask yourself as you design a framed page:

▶ How is this information organized? Is there a common set of options that people return to again and again?

▶ How will people navigate through the layers in the site? Will there be repeated elements—a table of contents? A set of buttons? A graphic?

▶ How are the elements related to each other? Do certain elements always appear together? Do certain elements control other elements?

▶ Are your readers using browsers that support frames? How will you structure a version of your site for those who aren't?

Frames versus Tables

You can use either frames or tables to create the effect of rows and columns on a page. A common mistake is to force a frames solution on a page when a clever use of tables would be the better solution. Both frames and tables have their own set of strengths.

Use tables when:

▶ You want an actual table on the page. For example, you have a set of quarterly results you want to show.

▶ Your page has many rows and columns. In most cases, a complex set of rows and columns is best handled with table tags.

▶ The row-and-column layout is unique to that page. In general, you'll only use frames when the layout and some of the content stay the same over many pages. If the layout appears on just that page, build it with table tags.

▶ You always want an entire page to repaint when someone accesses any part of it. The strength of frames is that a frame's content stays on the screen. If you want it to repaint anyway, tables might be a better technology for your page.

▶ A large percentage of your audience uses browsers that don't support frames. It almost goes without saying, but just in case—think about the people in your audience and what they are able to access as you design your site. If they're coming to you from AOL, for example, don't use frames. Create the effect with tables.

Use frames when:

▶ One section of the page remains relatively constant. A framed section downloads, paints once, and stays displayed.

▶ You want a cause-and-effect relationship between sections. With frames, you can click on an item in one frame and have something appear in another frame. No other HTML tag lets you create this type of relationship.

▶ The items in the tables and rows are in separate files. With frames, you can display the contents of multiple files on the same page at one time.

▶ There are a limited number of rows or columns on the page, and the same layout is repeated throughout most of your site. Frames are a good application when consistency is part of your goal.

Framed Applications

Most frame problems and complaints about sites that use frames fall into one of three categories:

▶ The site uses frames just to create the effect of rows and columns. Tables do this better and cleaner.

▶ The site jams lots of little frames onto the page. The idea seems to be that if two frames are good, seven are better. More than two or three frames creates a very cluttered page. There's so much noise and so many things going on that your readers will often just give up.

▶ The site goes into a sort of graphics-overload mode, with its creators thinking for some reason that using frames means you can use lots and lots of graphics.

It's not clear why people make that connection, but frames download just like any other HTML page. Graphics in frames take just as long to download and paint on the screen as graphics without frames. If you have two frames, each containing a file with lots of graphics, the reader actually perceives the page as taking twice as long to load.

In fact, frames are best used in relatively simple designs. Typically, they have no more than two horizontal and two vertical divisions. Some of the best uses of frames divide the screen into only two parts. Often, one of the frames will contain a set of buttons or a table of contents. This frame will seldom vary. It lets readers know what is part of the site and makes it easy for them to jump from one part to another.

Figure 8.2 shows another example of frames used well. The site "In Our Path" uses frames to show a thumbnail gallery. There are just two simple frames, but the effect works well with the content.

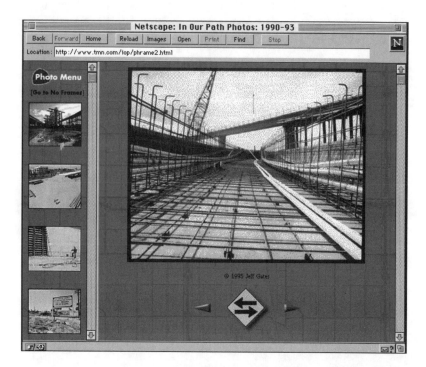

Figure 8.2
A simple but effective use of frames in the "In Our Path" site.

framesets—
A set of frame definitions.

BUILDING FRAMES

Frames are a little like server-side imagemaps in that you must first define the frames in one file and then actually use them in another file. You'll create one file that defines the framesets. This file will not contain any of your site's content; it just defines the frames, their names, and what content they will initially display. Your regular HTML text file includes a tag that tells the content to display inside one of the defined frames.

The browser gets pointed at an HTML file that contains frameset information. It opens the file, sees how to divide the page, gets a pointer to a content file, and displays the content in the appropriate frame.

Creating the Frameset File

The frameset defines each frame's size, name, and contents. Each frameset can either define a group of vertical frames or a group of horizontal frames. Framesets can be nested within each other, which is how you create a page with both horizontal and vertical divisions.

Before you build your frameset, you need to know what your framed page is going to look like. Specifically, you need to know:

▶ The number of columns or rows you want

▶ The depth, in pixels or as a percent of the browser window, each will be

▶ What content will first appear in those columns or rows

Sketch this information out on paper before you begin, and it will make the process of building frames much easier.

The HTML file that holds the frameset definition can contain up to five frame-related tags.

The frameset tag, <frameset>, starts the frameset definition. This tag defines the number and size of frames on the page. Each frameset can define either columns or rows and has two possible switches:

<frameset>—
Starts a frameset definition.

▶ *Cols.* Defines the number of vertical frames and the size of each

▶ *Rows.* Defines the number of horizontal frames and size of each

TIP: *You cannot define both rows and columns within the same frameset. If you want both rows and columns, you'll need to nest framesets.*

You use both switches the same way. After the equals sign, enter a quotation mark. Then, type the size of the first column or row. You can specify it in pixel units, as a percentage of the screen, or as an asterisk (*), which means that, after all other columns or rows are built, this column or row fills the remaining space. For example, the following tag sets a first column of 100 pixels and a second column that fills the remainder of the browser window:

```
<frameset cols="100,*">
```

If you are specifying the frame as a percentage, follow the percent number with a percent sign, as in 40%.

```
<frameset rows="60%,10%,*">
```

TIP: *As a general rule, it is a good idea to make the frame that will contain your fixed contents a specific size. That way, you know, for example, that your table-of-contents buttons will always fit correctly and be visible.*

<frame>—Defines a specific frame.

The frame tag, <frame>, describes each individual frame. Each frame in your frameset has its own separate frame tag. The first frame tag the browser encounters will be applied to the first column/row in the frameset tag. The second will apply to the second, and so on.

The frame tag has six switches:

▶ *Source* (type *src*) is the content file that the browser puts into this frame when it first displays the page. Typically, the file is an HTML file, but it could also be a GIF file, a PDF file, or another content file. The filename should always be surrounded by quotation marks.

▶ *Name.* Assigns a name to this frame so that you can specify it elsewhere and take action to it or with it.

▶ *Marginwidth.* Lets you specify a distance in pixels between the sides of the frame and the start of the text or graphics in the framed file.

▶ *Marginheight.* Lets you specify a distance in pixels between the top and bottom of the frame and the start of the text or graphics in the framed file.

- ▶ *Scroll.* Lets you control whether or not your reader sees the scroll bar in the frame. If you don't include this switch, the default is *auto*—that is, the scroll bar will appear only when there is content that extends beyond the size of the frame. A *yes* value always puts the scroll bar on the frame; a *no* value never puts the scroll bar on the frame. In general, you should just use the default.

- ▶ *Noresize.* Prevents your readers from resizing the frame. Normally, a person can click on the space between two frames and drag the divider bar to resize the frame. Most people don't do this, but if you want to ensure that they can't do it, include the noresize switch in your frame definition.

The tag </frameset> ends the frameset definition.

The tag <noframe> tells the browser how to display the page if the browser doesn't support frames. Between the noframe and end noframe tags you'll have a regular HTML file, starting and ending with a body tag. This is what readers whose browsers don't support frames will see.

Predictably, the tag </noframe> ends the no-frame section.

Following is the frameset HTML file we use for one of the Developer Zone pages, another page in which we employ frame features. We'll use it as an example as we walk through the steps in creating a framed document. The frame tags are marked in bold. Figure 8.3 shows what the page looks like in a browser window.

</frameset>—
Ends a frameset definition.

<noframe>—
Starts the unframed HTML page description.

</noframe>—
Ends the unframed HTML page description.

```
<html>
<head>
<title>Project Cool: More HTML</title>
</head>
<frameset cols="100,*">
<frame src="toc-advanced.html" name="tocframe" marginwidth="0"
marginheight="0">
< frame src="alchemy/01-moreintro.html" name="content">
</frameset>
```

```
<noframe>
<body bgcolor="000000" link="d2691e" vlink="d2691e" text="cccccc">
<p align=center>
<img src="images/amenu1.gif" width=75 height=91 alt="Rocket Fuel">
<a href=alchemy/01-moreintro.html><img src=images/amenu2.gif
width=75
height=29 border=0 alt="Adding Richness"></a>
<a href=alchemy/02-imagemap.html><img src= images/amenu3.gif
width=75
height=29 border=0 alt="Imagemaps"></a>
<a href=alchemy/03-tables.html><img src=img src=images/amenu4.gif
width=75 height=29 border=0 alt="Tables"></a>
<a href=alchemy/04-frames.html><img src=images/amenu5.gif width=75
height=29 border=0 alt="Frames"></a>

<p align=center>
This page is designed for maximum viewing pleasure under Frames.
<p align=center>
Click on one of the table of contents topics to continue.
<p align=center>
Copyright 1996<br>
Project Cool, Inc.<br>
All Rights Reserved<br>
</body>
</noframe>
</html>
```

To create a frameset file:

1. Start the frameset file as you would start any other HTML file, with an html tag and a header.

Figure 8.3
A framed page.

2. Create the frameset by typing the frameset tag. Remember, the frameset tag replaces the usual body tag.

```
<frameset
```

3. Complete the frameset tag, defining how many frames are on the page and what their sizes are. In this example, we have created two columns, one with a fixed width of 100 pixels and another that fills the rest of the browser window.

```
<frameset cols="100,*">
```

4. Define each frame with a frame tag. In this example, the first frame, which is 100 pixels wide, is called "tocframe" and contains a table-of-contents file with graphical buttons. The second frame, which will fill the rest of the browser window, is named "content." When it first appears, it will display the first chapter of the tutorial.

```
<frameset cols="100,*">
<frame src="toc-advanced.html" name="tocframe" marginwidth="0"
marginheight="0">
<frame src="alchemy/01-moreintro.html" name="content">
```

5. End the frameset definition with the end-frameset tag.

```
<frameset cols="100,*">
<frame src="toc-advanced.html" name="tocframe" marginwidth="0"
marginheight="0">
<frame src="alchemy/01-moreintro.html" name="content">
</frameset>
```

6. Create the no-frames section. Start it with the tag <noframe>; end it with the tag </noframe>. Remember, the no-frame section will include a body tag, just like a regular HTML page.

That's all there is to setting up a frameset file. The next step is to put content into the frames.

Frame Content

Creating the frames is the first step. Now that you've defined them, you can place any file inside them. You do this by adding one simple tag to your HTML file: <base>.

<base>—Sets a target frame.

For a moment, let's look at the way a regular, nonframed HTML page works. You type in a URL and the page appears on your screen, inside your browser window. Within the page are links to other pages. When you click on one of these links, the linked page replaces the current page in the window. The full browser window is the target location for the linked page.

Now let's look at a framed document. If you don't add any extra tags, each frame will work like a separate browser window. Click on a link inside that frame, and the contents of the frame will be replaced with the new, linked page.

But with frames, you can override this default action. When you put a document into a frame, you can tell the browser to display linked pages not in the same frame, but in another one. That's why you can click on an item in a table of contents and have the chapter appear in another frame, leaving the table of contents on the screen, untouched.

You create this effect by including the tag <base> into any HTML file. This tag tells the browser that it won't automatically display linked files in the same window.

The base tag has one switch: *target.*

The value of this switch is the name (in quotes) of the frame into which the browser will display linked files. Remember that you named each frame as part of the frame tag in your frameset? Well, you'll use these names to tell the browser where to display the files that are linked from the current file.

In our Developer Zone example, we created two frames: one for the table of contents and one for pages that change depending on what item the reader selects in the table of contents. The file that goes into the first frame is our actual table-of-contents file. Within that table-of-contents file, we told the browser that the target frame was the frame named "content." When you click on a table-of-contents button linked to another file, you see the new file—but you don't see it overwriting the table of contents itself. You see the new file in the second frame.

You can use multiple base tags in the same HTML file. When the HTML file reaches a link, it places the linked file or content in the target specified by the base tag that most closely precedes the link. So, if you want to send the contents of link *A* into frame *A* and the contents of link *B* into frame *B,* you'd set a base tag with the target of frame *A*. Then you'd create the link. A little further on down the file, you'd set a base tag with a target of frame *B* and create the next link.

Here's our table-of-contents file. As you can see, it looks like a normal HTML file, except for the addition of the base tag (in bold):

```
<html>
<head></head>
<base target="content">
<body bgcolor="000000" link="d2691e" vlink="d2691e">
<p align=center>
<img src="images/amenu1.gif" width=75 height=89 alt="Rocket
Fuel"> ...
```

OTHER BASE-TAG APPLICATIONS

Most of the time, your target frame will be the name of one of the frames in your frameset. However, there are a few other values you can use. Some of these you can use in an unframed area to create special effects.

Making a New Window

If you want the browser to open a new window, set the target value to be the name of frame that doesn't exist. To remember what you've done, you might want to make the name something like "new" or "anotherwindow." For example, when you click on links in a file that contains this base tag, the browser opens a new window for the linked page and leaves the current page on the screen:

```
<base target="newpage">
```

TIP: *You can use this tag in a file even when you aren't using frames. It's a nice little shortcut for creating a new window on your readers' screens.*

Overwriting the Frame

Every now and then, you may want the framed file to be replaced with another file. For example, you might have an index you want to display. When people click on the index link, you'd like the table of contents to disappear and be replaced with the index. To do this, set your target switch to equal "_self." For example:

```
<base target="_self">
```

TIP: *Don't forget to include the underscore before the word self.*

Filling the Full Page

You can have the linked page fill the entire browser window, overwriting all frames. To do this, you set the target switch to "_top," like this:

```
<base target="_top">
```

TIP: *Don't forget to include the underscore before the word top.*

Filling the Frameset

If you are using nested frames, you might want to use this setting from time to time. It places the linked page into the current frameset, overwriting all frames within the set. To do this, set the target switch to "_parent," like this:

```
<base target="_parent">
```

TIP: *If you have only one frameset, the result will be identical to setting the switch to "_top."*

NESTED FRAMES

Remember, each frameset can specify only columns or rows. So when you want both vertical and horizontal frames on your page, you must nest framesets within framesets.

The mechanics of nesting frames is quite simple. The complex part is designing the frames and their relationship with each other. Figure 8.4 shows a page with nested frames; the following is the code that created it.

```
<frameset cols="33%,33%,*">
<frame src="chapter1.html" name="colA">
  <!nested frame for center column>
  <frameset rows="33%,33%,34%">
  <frame src="character1.html" name="rowB1">
  <frame src="character2.html" name="rowB2">
  <frame src="character3.html" name="rowB3">
  </frameset>
<frame src="credits.html" name="colC">
</frameset>
```

As you do with nested tables, add extra space and comment lines in your HTML file to set off the nested items. This makes your file easier to debug and edit.

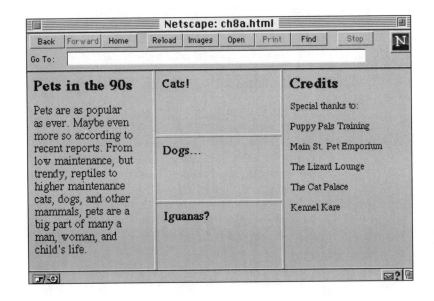

Figure 8.4
Nested vertical and horizontal frames.

To nest frames:

1. Create your first frameset. Define either rows or columns.

```
<frameset cols="33%,33%,*>
```

TIP: *Typically, the one you define first will be dictated by your design. In this example, we define columns first, because the full-length column is the first item on the page. This frameset divides the page into three columns.*

2. Define the first frame in the frameset. In this example, this frame is the first vertical column. It will contain the file "chapter1.html" and is named "colA."

```
<frame src="chapter1.html" name="colA">
```

3. Define the second frame in the frameset. The second frame is the second vertical column. But wait, this column is really three rows. Instead of defining it with a frame tag, we'll define it with a nested frameset that defines the three rows:

```
<frameset rows="33%,33%,34%">
```

4. Define each of the rows that is part of the nested frameset.

```
<frameset rows="33%,33%,34%">
<frame src="character1.html" name="rowB1">
<frame src="character2.html" name="rowB2">
<frame src="character3.html" name="rowB3">
```

5. End the nested frameset by typing the end-frameset tag:

```
<frameset rows="33%,33%,34%">
<frame src="character1.html" name="rowB1">
<frame src="character2.html" name="rowB2">
<frame src="character3.html" name="rowB3">
</frameset>
```

6. Define the remaining frame or frames as normal. In this example, we type a frame tag for the third and final column:

```
<frame src="credits.html" name="colC">
```

7. End the first frameset with its matching end-frameset tag.

```
<frame src="credits.html" name="colC">
</frameset>
```

As with nested tables, make sure that each start-tag has a corresponding end-tag and that each element in both the original and the nested items is defined. Remember, adding extra space, using comment lines, and setting off the nested tables will really help you ensure that all end-tags and items are in place.

Frames really aren't that difficult. Don't be afraid to experiment. Even if you end up not using them, they are an excellent way to think through your site and discover how the parts can be related.

JEFF GATES, FOUNDER, EYE TO I, WASHINGTON D.C.: IN OUR PATH

(http://www.tmn.com/iop/index.html)

Information Flow and Artists' Roles

It started out innocently enough, as a standard exhibit in traditional gallery space. It was to document, through photos and essays, the building of Los Angeles' Century Freeway. But artist/photographer Jeff Gates thought it could be more. By the time he was done, he had not only made powerful images of a process that transformed a neighborhood into a highway, but had created an interactive space where photography and community input came together to tell the story of a place, a time, and a construction project. The resulting site is called "In Our Path."

"I got great joy out of taking the information—essays and photos—and being able to make nonlinear connections and reconfigure the work in a hypermedia way. I wanted to see if I could take this exploration, encourage participation, and create a feedback area where people could express themselves. I'm interested in how

(continued on page 149) ▶

Figure 8.5
Home page of "In Our Path."

(continued from page 148)

artists can get involved in public issues," says Gates.

The "In Our Path" Web site is an example of the virtue of balance. Graphics without graphic overload. A story with community input. A clear path through the content without pressure to take a single route. As a site, "In Our Path" is a wonderful example of well-thought-out information flow, as well as an exploration of how art and community can meet in a gallery without walls.

This balance isn't accidental. In fact, it is at the center of Gates' Web philosophy. "The bottom line in Web design is balance—between content, information flow, and technology," he explains.

(continued on page 150) ▶

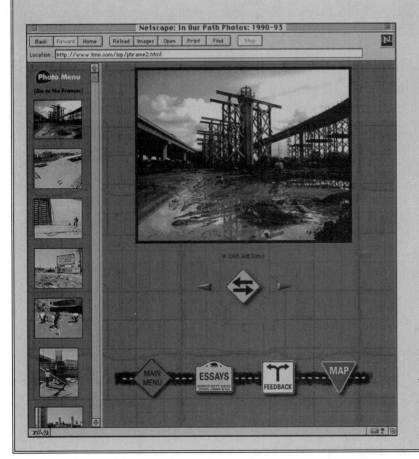

Figure 8.6
A second-level page from "In Our Path" balances browsing and detail.

(continued from page 149)

Gates, 46, now lives in the Washington, DC area and has founded a design firm, Eye to I. But he didn't start out as either a computer person or a graphic designer. He found the Web as an artist and photographer. His first computer experience came with the Macintosh in 1984, and he "was totally blown away by it," he recalls. He found the Web in 1995 and was instantly hooked by the possibilities.

"The thought of putting my work on the Net, where a potential 340 million people could view it, to have my work come in contact with an audience that might not be able see it in a traditional art setting, was wonderful and amazing for me," he says.

Artists ignore the Web at their own peril, he says, for the Web has the potential to be a transforming technology for the world of the creative person and his or her place in society. "In Our Path" is an example of how the artist and the process of art can again connect to the community.

"In the agricultural age, the artists were cultural spiritual givers. In the industrial age, artists were separated from the product of art and the process of art. In the information age, artists can reposition and reconnect with the process of art as both creators and interpreters. If we don't get our foot in the door, the Disneys and the Time Warners will take [the Web] and turn it into another passive form of entertainment with little true interaction."

LOW-BANDWIDTH DESIGN

A word of advice here. This is the most important chapter in the book. If you read nothing else (<grin> and we can't imagine you doing that </grin>), read this chapter! It could save your site.

Low bandwidth is a misunderstood concept on the Web. A lot of people think that it's just a matter of making everything smaller or using no graphics at all. That might help literal bandwidth, but it doesn't help your site become a better one, and it's really not the best approach. There are ways to build high-impact, low-fat Web sites. And that's what this chapter is all about.

low-bandwidth design—Using assorted techniques to minimize the download time of a Web page.

perceived speed—The speed at which a reader thinks a page downloads.

PERCEPTION

A big part of designing an effective Web site is understanding the way people experience the site. We can create two pages, each with the same approximate size and load time, and we bet that we can make you think one loaded much faster than the other. That's the real secret of low-bandwidth Web design: fooling the user into thinking your site is faster. It's all a matter of perception and perceived speed.

If readers think your site is fast, then it *is* fast. Perception creates reality. Conversely, if they think a site is slow, then they may not come back. It doesn't matter if you can time the load speed and "prove" that the fast and slow sites load at the same time—opinion has been formed, and that opinion becomes fast, regardless of what the second hand on the clock says.

Can you afford to have a site that feels slow? Speed is even important if everyone in your audience uses high-speed Internet connections. The faster you can make your site appear to respond, the happier the people who browse it will be, and the better your site will be received.

To make a site that is perceived as low-bandwidth, you need to think about how a user perceives your site. What can you do to make the site *feel* faster? Of course, you'll also want to do whatever you can to make your graphics tighter and more efficient; we'll show you how to do that in this chapter, too.

Many different factors influence speed of a Web site. One of the first things to remember is that speed is not what it claims to be on the Internet. A reader using a 28.8 modem may very well be surfing at a much lower speed, slower than even 14.4 baud. Traffic levels, telecommunication line quality, connection quality, and a host of other infrastructure issues can slow a Web site. These factors are beyond your control, and nothing in your design can change them, but it is important to be aware that just because you think your readers all have 28.8 modems doesn't mean they are literally accessing data at 28.8.

The type of computer your reader is using has an impact on site speed as well. A page loads and displays much faster on a Pentium than on a 468 PC—even if both machines have a 28.8 modem and a clean connection to the Net. The amount of memory the computer has also impacts the speed at which a page displays. The browser makes a difference, too. We have noticed that on certain machines, certain browsers display the same information faster than other browsers. Within corporations, the way a network is set up influences speed. We remember a certain T1 line that felt like a dial-in connection because of the way the internal network had been configured.

You can see that there are many factors that influence bandwidth in additional to the literal size of the information pipeline. And, unless you plan to personally supply every reader with a complete computer set-up, these factors are beyond your control. What is important as a Web builder is to understand that speed is about more than a type of telecommunications connection, and always plan for the bandwidth-eating gremlins in your design.

ONE SECOND, ONE K

Consider this: You've got a great-looking image for your front page. It has all the information that users need to navigate your site. It's a GIF that's 48K in size. On a modem, it takes 48 seconds to load that image. That's right, 48 seconds. It had best be one truly spectacular image.

The defense "but all my readers have ISDN" isn't worth all that much. Remember, the state of the Net, the reader's computer, and many other factors nibble away at bandwidth. Maybe your readers do get the image in less than 48 seconds. But is it worth waiting even 20 seconds for it? Try holding your breath as you watch the clock on your computer and count off 20 seconds—it feels a lot longer than it sounds.

TIP: *Allow one second for each kilobyte (K) of information to be transmitted over a modem: 60K of data = 1 minute of delay.*

ILLUSIONS OF SPEED

You know how long that graphic will take to download, but you really, *really* like it and still want to use it. What can you do about an image like that? Our solution would be to break it down into sections so that different pieces seem to load at the same time. While it will still take the same amount of time to transfer, the user sees different pieces coming in at once and perceives it as coming in faster. You might do something as simple as slicing the image into horizontal sections that load one at a time, creating a seamless graphic from many smaller pieces. You can achieve this effect using the pseudo-imagemapping techniques from Chapter 7.

TIP: *Divide large graphics into smaller slices to give your readers the illusion of a faster-loading image.*

While we are on the subject of loading images, there is one simple thing you can do that dramatically speeds up your site's apparent bandwidth. Every time you use an image tag, always specify its dimension using the width and height switches.

With this one simple addition, you have given the browser the ability to completely lay out the page before it has received all the image data. The browser will use a place holder for the image and flow the text around it, making your reader think the page is loading faster. You've now given the users something to do while the page's graphics load; they can start reading your page and even select an option from it. You've increased the apparent bandwidth of your pages, even though the total transfer still takes the same amount of time.

TIP: *Rule of Thumb: Always use width and height switches in the <img> tag.*

CATCHING CACHE

Modern browsers store the images for a Web page in a cache. This is a temporary storage area where frequently used pages and images are kept so that they don't have to be transferred again the next time they are needed. During a

apparent bandwidth—
The illusion of more content at a faster speed.

cache—A method of computer data storage.

Web session, two caches are typically in use: a memory cache and a disk cache.

The disk cache is a more permanent storage area. It holds images that will be used from session to session, even after you've exited your browser. When a browser accesses a page for which it has cached images, it doesn't need to transfer those images again over the Net; it simply pulls them up from the hard-drive cache and redisplays them. This process is quick and painless and works quite well for people who are visiting the same pages often.

The memory cache is only active for the current session and stores the last used images for nearly instant recall. This can be immensely useful if you know how to take advantage of it.

Take a look at the image in Figure 9.1. It is a company logo that serves as a header for a particular section of the company's Web site. It is a common practice to have this type of graphic within a site to provide a consistent look and feel. As you can see, both logos are remarkably similar. The only different is the division name: One logo is for Services division, and the other is for the Products division.

Standard practice would call for the production of two logos, one for each page. But if you look closely, you'll notice that there is only one part of the image that changes: division name. What happens, then, if we break the logo down into two distinct sections? In this case, one graphic

Figure 9.1
Logos used in a Web site's section header.

Figure 9.2

A commonly used element can be split into its own file. In this example, the logo and the division name become separate pieces. The browser can cache the logo and use it over and over, saving download time.

would be the main logo by itself and the other would be the division name. Figure 9.2 shows how that could be accomplished with this logo.

Dividing this image into two pieces allows us to reuse the logo section on every Web page. Because the logo section would be in the memory cache of the user's browser, it would appear to load very quickly on the page. Download time is minimized, because only the division-name graphic needs to download. Suddenly, you've created subpages with unique graphics that load in much less time than before. If you construct the images using pseudo-imagemap techniques, they'll look like one seamless graphic to your reader.

TIP: *When one part of a graphic is reused throughout the site, break it out into its own file and reuse it over and over again, taking advantage of the browser's cache.*

Reusing graphics within your site allows you to build more graphically rich pages without the load-time overhead that would occur if you were using only original graphics on each page. If you add more original graphics as a reader descends into your site and reuse previously loaded images, with careful planning you can have some very effective and elaborate graphic-intensive pages that remain low-bandwidth, because most of the images are already cached.

OPTIMIZING IMAGES

The next important thing you can do is to optimize your images. Optimizing your graphics reduces page load time and increases apparent bandwidth.

Graphics can make a page more attractive and easier to use, but they also dramatically increase the size of the file and the time it takes readers to download it. Striking a balance between load time and graphic design has been the headache of many a Web designer. Happily, there are many ways to find that balance.

Some people interpret the idea of low-bandwidth as "ban all graphics." That would be a terrible loss. The Web is a visual medium, and graphics can add a great deal of value. The trick is to keep a graphic's look and feel while slimming down its overhead. This isn't at all difficult to do.

Selecting the Right Format

There are two common graphic standards on the Web: GIF and JPEG. Matching the right format with the right image can save valuable megabytes and make your images display better. Here are a few rules of thumb for selecting graphic formats:

▶ If the image has large areas of solid color, GIF format is best.

▶ If the image is photo-realistic, use a JPEG format.

▶ If it's a combination, try both alternatives and see which gives you the best fit in terms of both file size and quality.

Like many others who work with graphics, we use Adobe's Photoshop to prepare our images for the Web. We have found it to be the best solution for us, and the examples we use refer to Photoshop. There are other programs on the market; if you are using one of these, adapt the Photoshop techniques to the commands specific to your graphics program.

JPEG Settings

Remember that your photo and photo-realistic images are going to be viewed on a computer screen—most likely a

72-dpi monitor. This means that when you scan in a photo, you don't need to scan at maximum resolution. We find that 100 dpi is usually adequate.

For people who are accustomed to working with print design, this will feel really unnatural at first. You'll probably worry about loss of quality, missing detail, and image deterioration. Don't worry about these things—the computer screen can't display those subtle details anyway, and it can make a low-resolution image seem sharp and crisp. The monitor is a completely different display medium than ink on paper.

Once you've done your touch-up or other image work, reduce the image to the size it will appear on your Web page. Again, this makes the file smaller.

The Quality Setting option in Photoshop gives you several ways to save a JPEG-formatted file. You can select poor, medium, or highest. The highest setting gives you the most quality, but also the largest file size. We've found that the medium setting is usually fine for most images intended to be viewed on a computer screen. However, avoid the poor setting. It does produce the smallest file, but the final image loses too much quality.

GIF Settings

When creating a GIF file, your final image size and quality are determined by how intelligently you make your indexed conversion choices. Indexed conversion is the process of changing the image from 24-bit color into an indexed palette, which is the table of colors used by GIF images.

With indexed conversion, the first thing to worry about is the image's bit depth. This determines how many colors are used in your final image as well as how much storage and display space the file's color index uses. Play with this setting using the Undo feature of Photoshop to determine the lowest number of colors you can use without sacrificing

indexed conversion—The process of changing an image from 24-bit color to an indexed palette.

indexed palette—The table of colors used by GIF images.

bit depth—Number of colors in an image.

image quality. We find that most images can be easily brought down to six or seven bits.

The next important factor is the type of palette you use. Image snobs that we are, we want as accurate a color representation as possible on our true-color displays. An adaptive color palette seems to work best for us. This give the greatest possible final image quality across the widest range of platforms. Other palette choices are not as flexible across platforms.

> **palette**—Range of available colors.

Your next decision is whether to use dithering. Dithering is a way of simulating a color by using alternating pixels of different colors. For example, dithering might simulate purple by putting a blue and red pixel next to each other. Dithering makes a smoother image with fewer color bands but remember that dithering increases file size. It will really depend on the particular image whether dithering is worthwhile.

> **dithering**—Simulating a color by using alternating pixels of different colors.

Using these tips to play with your image in Photoshop can significantly reduce final image size without sacrificing image quality. When you save the final Web version of your graphic, save it at the size it will be used on the Web page. This reduces overhead and computer processing time.

One more important factor for designers to remember is that your eye is much more critical of your final product than your readers' eyes are. Sometimes you can spend too much time trying to make things absolutely perfect. Try to find the best compromise of quality versus file size. Getting a quality image is important, but you may go so far to the extreme that no one will be waiting around to see it by the time it finally downloads.

Low-bandwidth design is mostly about taking advantage of the way the Web works to maximize your impact without excessive overhead. It's not difficult, and the results are rewarding—both for you and your readers who are awed at how fast your site works.

(www.crayola.com)

Dancing between Design and Technology

Crayola describes itself as "colorful and fun"—and its Web site cleanly brings that image through. Crayola's site, created by Anabella Wewer for Binney & Smith, is among the best examples of branded, corporate Web sites. It's a great example of how look and feel can carry across different media. Even small details—the use of crayons and markers as navigational buttons, for example—tie the pieces together. It is said that the devil is in the details. That may be true—but so is the secret of a cohesive Web site.

(continued on page 161) ▶

Figure 9.3
*Crayola's
home page.*

(continued from page 160)

It's not surprising that Wewer, 31, began her career working in print, designing direct-marketing and collateral projects for an agency in Boston. Those design skills combined with her understanding of technology have resulted in a slew of exceptional Web work.

"I'm a designer first, and I happen to produce things for the Web," she says of her philosophy. "I also do print, and I do multimedia. Web design isn't something you can single out. I design business cards, but I don't go around calling my self a 'business-card designer.' The Web's not different—it's just a different medium."

Crayola had some clear goals when it created its Web presence. Its focus wasn't on selling product but on creating a channel for customer communication and extending its brand image (see Figure 9.4). (continued on page 162) ▶

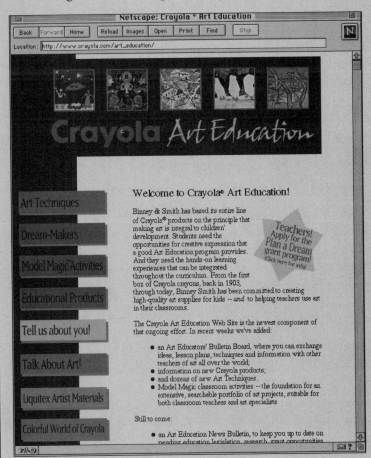

Figure 9.4
There's no question that this page belongs to the Crayola family.

(continued from page 161)

"We see it as an adjunct to our 800-number service" says Crayola spokesperson Brad Drexler. "It's a cost-effective means of communication. We get requests for stain-removal tips, company history, and background . . . a lot of the requests that we get through our 800 center are now directly addressed on our Internet site. That lets us reach a greater volume of consumers."

Two audiences Crayola wanted to reach were children and art educators; the Web provided a structure for these groups that couldn't be duplicated in another medium.

"It allows them to communicate directly to the end user," says Wewer. "When the end user is kids, that means making it fun. And the Web can do that well—things that move and jump and talk to them are fun.

"Plus the interactive features of the Net get people involved. We have a news group (in the Art Educator area) that lets people communicate with each other without intervention. It's immediate gratification, and people seem to like that," she says.

Features like rotating art galleries and interactive chat (both part of the Crayola site) cry out for a Web builder who understands technology as well as design—and not just HTML tags, but the underlying demands of the technology. Wewer is fortunate that her Easton, PA-based company, Black Box, has two sister companies rooted in the technological side of the Web. Oasis is an ISP, and Renaissance Integration does customer programming and database applications. Wewer worked with Renaissance to create a form engine that makes the threaded conversation in Art Educators friendly and easy to use. This company also provided a statistics engine that directs usage feedback to Crayola's marketers, helping them know where to focus development energies.

The bottom line of the dance between technology and design? Says Wewer, "If the design is cool but it doesn't work technologically, then the site doesn't work for anyone."

10
PREPARING FORMS

There comes a time when everyone wants to add a form of some sort to a Web page. Maybe it's a just-for-fun guest book where people can jot down their names and comments. Maybe it's a form that lets readers give you structured feedback. Or maybe it's an order entry form for your products. Forms are a way of using one of the strengths of the online medium—two-way communication—to add functionality to your Web site. Forms allow you to pass information, both hidden and visible, to a program on a Web server. Text areas, radio buttons, check boxes, and selection menus are all part of the options for input with HTML forms.

There are two parts to a form:

▶ The first is the graphical form your readers see and enter data into. Building this form is a fairly straightforward process involving a few new HTML tags that define field types. This chapter teaches you how to build a custom HTML form.

▶ The second is the program that processes the form data. These programs are custom-built for each form and reside on your server. It's beyond the scope of this book to teach you the programming to make Common Gateway Interface (CGI) forms processing work. If you

> **form**—A way to pass information from a Web browser to a program on a Web server.
>
> **field**—A place in a form to enter information or request an action.

Common Gateway Interface (CGI)—A way of connecting a program to a Web form.

aren't a programmer yourself, you'll want to work with someone who understands the Common Gateway Interface and can program in Perl, C, tcl, shell, Visual Basic, AppleScript, Frontier, or another language that supports CGI.

DESIGNING A FORM

Forms appear on your Web site for a purpose. There is some information you want to gather and use. So it only follows that you want to design a form that makes the process easy and inviting. "Hah!" you might think. "Forms are just a bunch of blocks and lines!" Actually, there is a bit more to form design than that. Over the years, companies have spent serious dollars designing forms that collect the necessary information while being easy to understand. If you think forms are easy, just think about your tax forms for a moment: good design or a painful effort to use?

Tips for Form Design

What's in a Form?

Before you create a form, spend some serious thought about what information you want to capture. Do you want a name or a last name? Do you want open-ended responses or a ranking on a scale of one to four? If you want a sales lead, what individual pieces of information are actually necessary to getting it? Ask yourself which items are essential and which fall into the nice-to-have-if-we-can category. When your programmer creates the program that interprets the form data, you can have it make some fields required—but if everything is required, people can become annoyed and just exit the form altogether.

Think about how the reader will perceive the form. It needs to be immediately obvious what information people need to enter where. Clarity and simplicity are critical in the form's design. No one particularly likes to fill out a form. If you have to pause to wonder: "Do they want my first name in this field or that field?" you may never finish the form.

In general, people respond more accurately (and you have more usable data) if they have choices to select. If you want to know someone's age, you might be better off with a set of radio buttons or a pulldown menu that offers five age categories. If the form involves a search, you can often make the process less frustrating by setting the search criteria fields as a set of checkbox options instead of a search string that readers have to type. For example, one field might offer the checkbox options "Movie," "Theatre," "Art," and "Sports;" and a second might offer "Monday," "Tuesday," "Wednesday," "Thursday," "Friday," "Saturday," and "Sunday." It's a lot easier for a reader to click on "Sports" and "Sunday" than to think about the proper thing to key in to find out what sport events are happening on Sunday.

Never assume anything! It's surprising what people do and don't do. At one point in time, we had a nomination form for our Coolest on the Web section. The form had a slot where people entered a URL, the category for which the site was nominated, some space for free text about why the site was cool, and the e-mail address of the respondent. Four simple fields, right? Less than half the responses included the category—we didn't explicitly say, "Select the category here."

The Importance of Words

Think about the actions or options available to your readers as they fill out the form. Are they *submitting* the information? Are they *buying* an item? Are they *checking* their status? Are they *applying* for membership? Are they *searching* for events in Montana in July? Verb choice is important in a form. It makes it clear to a reader what he or she is doing or setting in motion by completing the form. You'll also want to put verbs on the action buttons that readers click. A compelling verb makes the reader understand that clicking on the button is an important part of filling the form. Which of the options in Figure 10.1 would be more likely to get a response?

The same holds true for the text near the fields. Use direct action commands wherever possible. For example:

▶ Click on a category.

▶ Type your last name.

▶ Enter your password.

Remember the Processing Needs

Talk to your programmers about how the data will be processed and what might make the processing easier. For

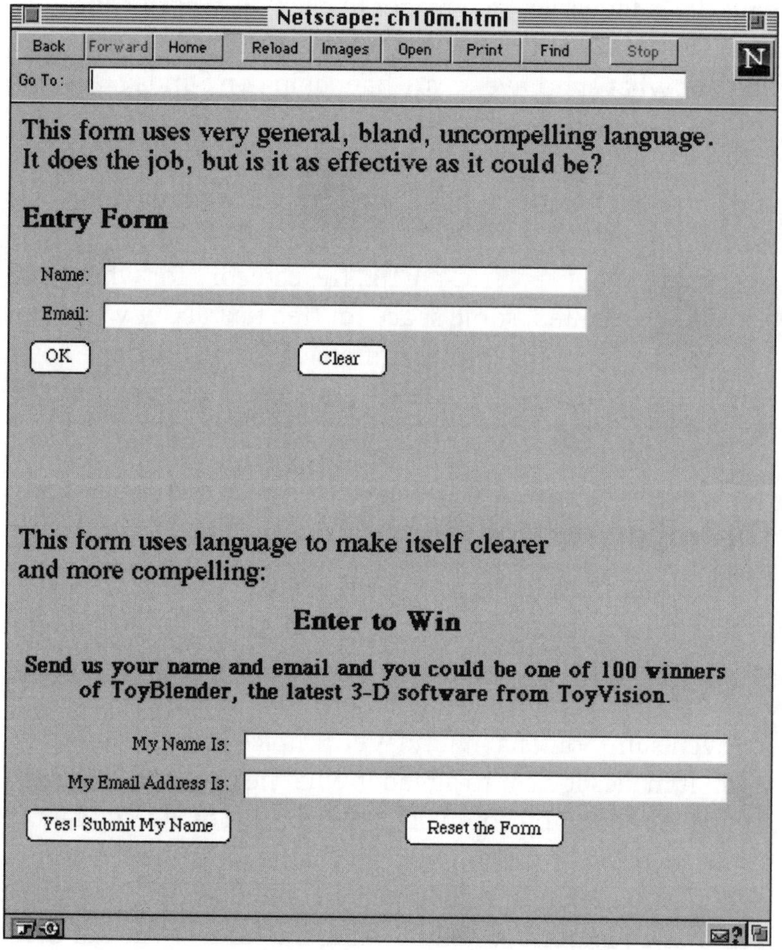

Figure 10.1
Two versions of the same form—only the text is different.

example, if you are collecting addresses, should each address line be a separate item? Do you want five or nine-digit ZIP codes? Are you looking for middle initials, and would those go in a separate field or as part of the first or last name? Is there some backend database that requires you to collect a specific bit of data, such as an item number from the catalog? Remember, collecting data in the form is just part of the process. Walking through what happens after you have the data can help you find bugs or holes early on, when they are easier to fix.

> **backend database**—A database that underlies an information or publishing process.

Remember Your Manners

What happens when the reader does something to produce an error, say to try and submit the form without entering a required field? As you create your form and think about how it will be processed, don't forget to think about error messages—what they'll say and how they'll look. People often take error messages personally. A cold, "Reenter name value" message doesn't encourage people to reenter the value. And it doesn't make them feel very good about your company, either.

Make error messages meaningful. Instead of saying the somewhat vague "Reenter name value," your message might say, "Please reenter your first name." Not only is this more pleasant, it is also clearer and more understandable.

Don't forget affirmation messages either. "Thanks for joining!" or "Welcome to the Club" are small things that can give your readers a nice little warm fuzzy and make them feel better about your site. After all, they did just do *you* a favor by completing a form. For example, when someone submits a sighting to our Daily Sighting section, we display the graphical thank-you note that you see in Figure 10.2. If you want to see this in action, go to http://www. projectcool.com/sightings, select the Submit a Sighting option, and complete the short submission form. We sometimes get one submission followed by several blank submis-

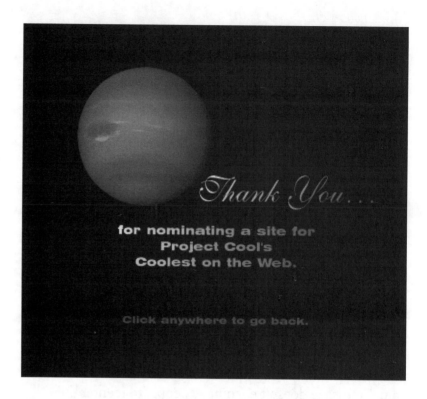

Figure 10.2
An affirmation message; this one thanks people for nominating a site.

sions from the same person and suspect that they are showing off the thank-you note.

Neatness Counts

Keep your forms legible and logical. They don't have to be works of art or acts of creative genius, but they do need to be neat and readable. If you can't be trusted to present a professional face in your form, why would readers trust you with their information? You can use tables to make forms line up neatly and cleanly. The last section of this chapter shows you an example of a form within a table.

Lay out the entries in a logical order. If someone has entered a first name, the next logical field would be last name. Don't jumble things up. It just confuses and annoys your reader—and confused or annoyed readers seldom complete forms.

BUILDING A FORM

The process of building an HTML form is fairly straightforward. It uses eight simple tags:

- ▶ The tag <form> starts the form
- ▶ The tag <input> creates a variety of form fields
- ▶ The tag <select> creates selection list fields
- ▶ The tag <option> creates a choice in the selection list field
- ▶ The tag </select> ends a selection list field
- ▶ The tag <textarea> creates a text area field
- ▶ The tag </textarea> ends the text area field
- ▶ The tag </form> ends the form.

TIP: *Remember, you can't use a form properly until a program to process it is in place on your server.*

Layout

The best way to control the layout of the form is by creating a table and inserting a field in each cell. The last section of this chapter shows you how tables and forms work together. If you do not use tables, your form will simply be one field after another, with only basic HTML formatting to break lines, as shown in Figure 10.3.

Additionally, you can use text and other standard HTML tags to create labels or instructions for your form and its fields.

Form Tags

There are eight form tags.

Like tables, a form begins with a start tag. In this case, the start tag is <form>. *Form* has two required switches:

<form>—Starts the form.

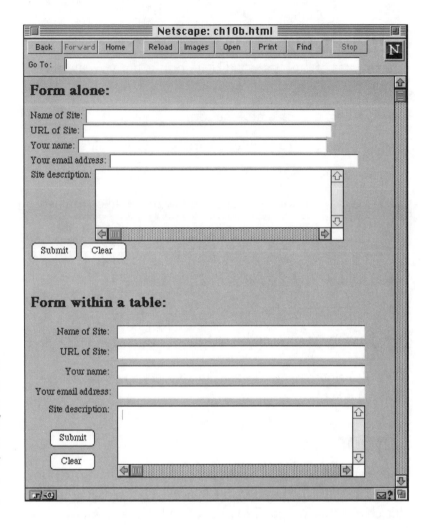

Figure 10.3
The difference between a form created with and without tables. Notice how the one without tables appears in one, uneven vertical row.

▶ *Method=get/post* tells the server how it will receive information. With the get option, the form information is passed visibly in the URL call, and your readers can see it in the location bar of the browser. The post method passes information invisibly.

TIP: *If you use the get method, people can bookmark their queries. For example, if your form lets readers search a database, it might be a good thing to allow them to bookmark the search.*

▶ *Action="program name"* identifies the location and name of the program that will process the forms data.

This program must reside on your Web server, usually within the cgi-bin directory.

Here's an example of a form tag that creates entries in a guest book:

```
<form method="post" action="/cgi-bin/guestbook.pl">
```

The tag <input> creates one field within a form. Your form will likely have multiple input tags. The input tag has two switches that must always be present. Additional switches are added for certain kinds of fields.

> ▶ *Name="variable name"* names the field. This name can be whatever you want it to be, *but*—and this is a very important but—the program on the server will be receiving this name as identification for the variable, and you should work with the programmer to make sure you are both naming each field the same thing. If you name the field "email" and your programmer calls it "e-mail," the form won't work properly.

> ▶ *Type=text/password/checkbox/radio/submit/reset/ image* defines the type of field.

The tag <select> starts the definition of a selection list field within the form. The field displays as either a pop-up menu or as a menu with slider bar. The select tag has three switches:

> ▶ *Name="variable name"* names the field.

> ▶ *Size=xx* describes the depth of the menu in screen rows. If you have more options than will fit in the menu window, a small scroll bar appears, and your readers can scroll through the options. If you omit the size switch, the field appears as a pop-up menu.

> ▶ *Multiple* lets readers make multiple selections from the list. If you include the multiple switch, the effect is somewhat like a checkbox. If you exclude it, the effect

<input>—Creates a variety of form fields.

variable—An item, the value of which changes.

<select>—Creates a selection-list field.

is like a radio button, in which only one option can be selected at a time.

The tag <option> creates a choice in a selection-list field.

The tag </select> ends the selection-list field.

The tag <textarea> creates a scrollable text field. This tag has three switches:

- *Name="variable name"* names the field.
- *Rows=xx* describes the depth of the field in screen rows.
- *Cols=xx* describes the width of the field in screen columns.

The tag </textarea> ends the text-area field.

The tag </form> ends a form. As with other functions, you must always have both a start and an end tag.

Fields

A form is made of a number of fields. Each field is a place where your reader can enter one piece of data. There are nine types of fields you can create. You will give each field a name, identify its type, and enter other values appropriate to that field.

These are the field types you create with the input tag:

- *Text.* Produces a text input box.
- *Password.* Produces a text input box. When you type in the box, the results display as asterisks (****) instead of as characters.
- *Checkbox.* Produces a field that reader clicks on to select.

<option>—
Creates a choice in a selection-list field.

</select>—Ends a selection-list field.

<textarea>—
Creates a text-area field.

</textarea>—
Ends a scrollable text field.

</form>—Ends the form.

checkbox—A selection that is turned on or off by clicking in a box. Multiple check-boxes can be turned on at the same time within a group of options.

- *Radio buttons.* Produces a field that is a series of options. Readers select the option they want by clicking on it. Clicking on one option turns off the others.

- *Submit.* Produces a button that, when clicked, sends the data in the form to the server.

- *Reset.* Returns all the fields to their default values.

- *Image.* Inserts a graphic that works like the submit button. Clicking on the image sends the data in the form to the server.

These are fields you create with other form tags:

- *Selection-list fields.* Produces a pop-up or scrolling menu of choices.

- *Text area.* Produces a scrolling text field for entering notes or comments.

Text

The text field is one of the most common field types. It creates a text-entry field. When you create a text field, you must also define its default size, the maximum number of characters it can hold, and its default value. To do this, you add the following switches to the input tag:

- *Size* (type *size=xx*)

- *Maximum length* (type *maxlength=xx*)

- *Value* (type *value="default"*)

For example, the following code produces the field shown in Figure 10.4. The text input box on the screen is 50 columns wide and will accept 50 characters maximum for input. It will contain a default value of "email@nowhere.com," which will appear in the field when the user loads the page. It will pass the input to the server in a variable called "emailaddress," which the server will use in the program to which the data is being passed.

radio buttons— A selection that is turned on or off by clicking in a toggle-switch circle. Only one radio button can be turned on at a time within a group of options.

Submit—To send something to the server for processing.

pop-up menu— A list of choices that appears (or pops up) only when your cursor touches a certain spot on the screen.

scrolling menu— A list of choices in a scrolling box.

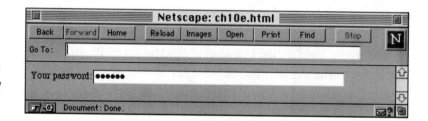

Figure 10.4
A text-input box.

```
<input name="emailaddress" type="text" size=50 maxlength=50
value"email@nowhere.com">
```

Password

The password field is really just another type of text field. It uses the same additional switches and behaves in the same way, except instead of displaying text in the field, it displays a series of asterisks. For example, this code produces the field shown in Figure 10.5. The password input box in this example is 50 columns wide and will accept 50 characters maximum for input. There is no default value.

```
<input name="password" type="password" size=50 maxlength=50>
```

Checkbox

The checkbox field produces a value with a checkbox in front of it. Readers select the value by clicking on the checkbox. You can set the default so that the box appears on the screen already checked or left empty. To do this, add the following optional switches to the input tag:

▶ *Value="value name".* If you don't include the value switch, the server assumes that the value is on when

Figure 10.5
*A password
input box.*

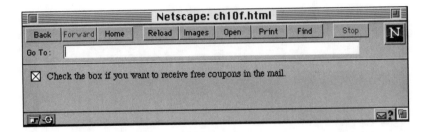

Figure 10.6
A checkbox field.

the box is checked and that there is no value at all when the box is unchecked.

▶ Checked. If you don't include the checked switch, the checkbox appears on the screen empty.

For example, the following code produces the field shown in Figure 10.6. The form's designer added HTML text for the directions. The checkbox's default value is to display a check mark, sending the on-value to the server.

```
<input name="includeme" type="checkbox" checked>
```

Radio Button

The radio button is ideal for multiple-choice questions. It is similar to the checkbox, except that it can be used with a group of values. When used with a group of values, it allows only one choice in the group to be selected.

When you create a radio-button group, you need to enter an input tag for each option. But all the tags share the same variable name with the name switch. The shared name tells the browser that they are part of the same group.

When you use radio buttons, you'll need to add one additional switch to the input tag that sets the button's value and have the option of adding a second that sets a default state: *value* (type *value="value name"*).

You can use the checked switch for radio buttons, too. If you don't include the checked switch, the radio button appears on the screen turned off.

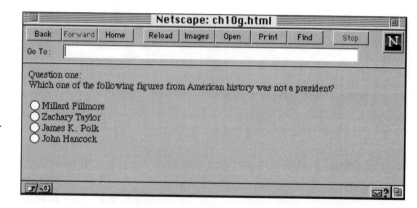

Figure 10.7
An example of radio buttons with a multiple-choice question.

This code produces the field shown in Figure 10.7.

```
Question one:<br>
Which one of the following figures from American history was not a
president?
<p>
<input name="question1" type="radio" value="Millard Fillmore">Millard
Fillmore<br>
<input name="question1" type="radio" value="Zachary Taylor">Zachary
Taylor<br>
<input name="question1" type="radio" value="James K. Polk">James K.
Polk<br>
<input name="question1" type="radio" value="John Hancock">John
Hancock<br>
```

Submit

Possibly the most important type of field is the submit field. After all, if you don't have a submit button, how can anyone submit information to the server?

You add one switch to the input tag when you create a submit button: *value="text in the button."*

```
<input name="submit" type="submit" value="Send Now">
```

Figure 10.8 shows what this button looks like. Notice that the text in the value switch appears in the button itself. You can put any message you like here, and you can even pad the edges with spaces to give some limited control over button size.

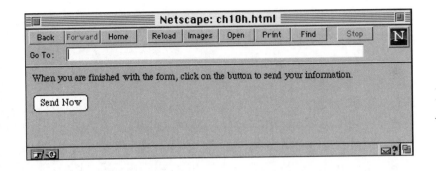

Figure 10.8
A submit button with the text value "Send Now."

Reset

You create a reset button in much the same way you create the submit button. When readers click on the reset button, all the fields in the form are reset to their default state.

You add one switch to the input tag when you create a reset button: *value="text in the button."*

```
<input name="reset" type="reset" value="Reset the Form">
```

Figure 10.9 shows what this button looks like. Notice that the text in the value switch appears in the button itself. You can put any message you like here, and you can even pad the edges with spaces to give some limited control over button size.

Image

The last input type is the image type, which lets you put your own image in the form in place of the standard submit button.

Figure 10.9
A reset button with the text value "Reset the Form."

You may add three additional switches to the input tag when you create an image button:

▶ *Source* (type *src="imagename"*) specifies the URL of the image, just as it does in the insert-image tag.

▶ *Border* (type *border=xxx*) creates a link border around the graphic, just as it does in the insert-image tag.

▶ *Align* (type *align=left/right*) aligns the image in the browser window, just as it does in the insert-image tag.

Using an image as a button is quite often a good choice, as it allows you to maintain a constant look and feel with your site. The following is an example of an image-input code, and the results are illustrated in Figure 10.10.

```
<input type="image" name="image" src="images/button.gif"
align=left border=0>
```

Selection List Field

Another type of field you can create is the selection-list field. You do not create it with the input tag, however. You create it with selection-list tags within the form.

The select tag, <select>, starts a selection-list field. It works a little like a regular list tag, in that you start it, note each option, and then turn it off. The select tag has three switches that define the field:

▶ *Name="variable name"* is the name the HTML form and the form program use to describe this field.

Figure 10.10
An image used in place of an HTML-generated submit button.

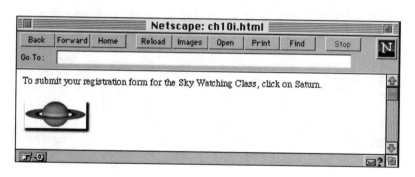

- *Size=xx* describes the depth of the menu in screen rows. If you have more options than will fit in the menu window, a small scroll bar appears, and your readers can scroll through the options. If you omit the size switch, the field appears as a pop-up menu. Figure 10.11 illustrates the difference.

- *Multiple* lets readers make multiple selections from the list. If you include the multiple switch, the effect is somewhat like a checkbox. If you exclude it, the effect is like a radio button, in which only one option can be selected at a time.

The option tag, <option>, creates a choice within the selection list. You type the tag, then type the option.

The tag </select> ends the multiple-choice menu field.

Here is an example of the select tag in action. In the first example, we create a menu with a slider bar, as seen in the top part of Figure 10.11. In the second, we create a pop-up menu, as seen in the bottom part of Figure 10.11.

```
<p align=center><b>Select One Color:</b>
<select name="choice" size="50">
<option>Blue
<option>Green
<option>Purple
<option>Yellow
</select>

<p align=center><b>Select One Size:</b>
<select name="size">
<option>Small
<option>Medium
<option>Large
<option>X-large
</select>
```

Scrollable Text Fields

Sometimes you need a large scrollable text field into which your readers can enter multiple lines of text. For example, you might set up a feedback or e-mail form and want to leave a space where readers can type a short note.

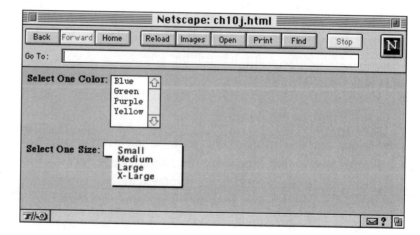

Figure 10.11
Different ways of offering multiple-choice menus.

The <textarea> tag creates a scrollable text field. It has three switches:

► *Name="variable name"* is the name both the HTML form and the form program use to describe this field.

► *Rows=xx* specifies the number of screen rows in the field, effectively setting the display depth of the field.

► *Cols=xx* specifies the number of screen columns in the field, effectively setting the width of the field.

The tag </textarea> ends the scrollable text field.

If you want default text in the box's typing area, simply include it between the tags <textarea> and </textarea>.

Figure 10.12 shows an example of a text-area field created by this code:

```
<textarea name="message" rows=4 cols=50>Enter your message
here!</textarea>
```

Creating the Form

To create a form:

1. Start the form tag:

```
<form
```

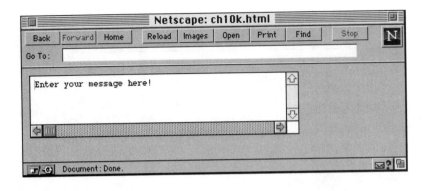

Figure 10.12
A text-area field that lets readers enter comments or notes.

2. Type the method by which the data in the form will be passed to the server. *Get* makes it visible; *post* makes it invisible. Remember to put quotation marks around the method value.

```
<form method="post"
```

3. Type the location and name of the form program on your Web server. Remember to put the URL in quotes.

```
<form method="post" action="/cgi-bin/guestbook.pl"
```

4. End the form tag.

```
<form method="post" action="/cgi-bin/guestbook.pl">
```

5. Enter each field value.

```
<form method="post" action="/cgi-bin/guestbook.pl">
<input name="address" type="text" size="50" maxvalue="100">
```

6. End the form with the end-form tag.

```
<form method="post" action="/cgi-bin/guestbook.pl">
<input name="address" type="text" size="50" maxvalue="100">
</form>
```

PUTTING THE FORM IN A TABLE

Now that you know what tags create the forms, it's time to give you some bad news. Forms are ugly. You'll notice when you build your first HTML form that nothing ever seems to line up. You can stick spaces here and there, insert breaks and so on. All to no avail. It's really tough to make a good-looking forms page with the form tags alone.

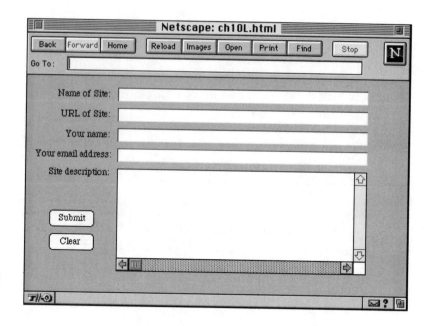

Figure 10.13
A form inside a table.

Now the good news. You *can* make great-looking forms pages. All you have to do is to put the form tags into a table. Then you can line everything up so that the form looks good. Here's the code to one of our forms in a table; Figure 10.13 shows you what it looks like online.

```
<FORM METHOD="POST" ACTION="/cgi-bin/s_submit.pl">
<table>
<tr>
<td align=right>Name of Site:</td>
<td><INPUT TYPE="text" NAME="sitename" SIZE="50" MAXLENGTH="100"></td>
</tr>
<tr>
<td align=right>URL of Site:</td>
<td><INPUT TYPE="text" NAME="url" SIZE="50" MAXLENGTH="100"
VALUE=""></td>
</tr>
<tr>
<td align=right>Your name:</td>
<td><INPUT TYPE="text" NAME="name" SIZE="50" MAXLENGTH="100"
VALUE=""></td>
</tr>
<tr>
<td align=right>Your email address:</td>
<td><INPUT TYPE="text" NAME="email" SIZE="50" MAXLENGTH="100"
VALUE=""></td>
</tr>
<tr>
```

```
<td valign op align=right>Site description:</td>
<td rowspan=3><TEXTAREA NAME="describe" ROWS=8 COLS=46></TEXTAREA>
</td>
</tr>
<tr>
<td valign=bottom align=center><INPUT TYPE="submit" NAME="submit"
VALUE=" Submit "></td>
</tr>
<tr>
<td valign op align=center><INPUT TYPE="reset" NAME="" VALUE="  Clear
"></td>
</tr>
</table>
</FORM>
```

Notice in the source code how we've used the align and valign switches to properly align everything. We've also made the text fields the same horizontal size. These tricks, although they'll vary from form to form, can give you a very professional look. Review the table tags and think of them as layout tools, and soon you'll be creating professional-looking forms that your Web friends will be copying.

CRASH SITE (www.crashsite.com)

A very long time ago, back in the pre-Web era, Ian Rogers was a student at the University of Indiana. He'd done a project at the music library turning hard-copy listings into digital ones, and he was trying to figure out how to deploy a program to search for these music objects across the library's mixed computer network. Mosaic had just emerged, and a friend suggested that maybe the best way to solve the music problem was to tie it to the Web as a Perl gateway. So he did.

"That was my first exposure to the Web," said Ian Rogers, who is now technical director for the Big Gun Project in Santa Monica. "We had no idea that the rest of the world would care about the Web. We did it as an internal project."

Now the world is very interested in what Rogers, 23, is doing on the Web. Big Gun's Crash Site (www.crashsite.com) is a sort of Generation-X culture clash: writing meets design meets cutting-edge Web technology. It's very cool in the way it combines breakthough creative thought with innovative technological underpinnings. Political e-zine Salvo (www.salvo.com) and cinema-on-the-internet FilmZone (www.filmzone.com) are two other sites also blessed with the Big Gun touch.

"Crash Site was the idea of Jim Evans, creative director at rVision [Big Gun's parent design firm]," says Rogers. "He sent me these maps (of the site plan) that were phenomenal. I've never seen a site that was so carefully planned. We were sitting in Indiana doing the programming for him, and as we were working we were thinking: This is incredible."

So how did Rogers move from the music library to Crash Site? Well, like most things on the Web, it wasn't a straight line. He's a Beastie Boys fan, and in some

(continued on page 185) ▶

(continued from page 184)

downtime between graduation and graduate school, he built a fan page. The Beastie Boys management company saw his work and, instead of screaming "cease and desist," asked him to do some additional work for the group. He was hooked. (continued on page 186) ▶

Figure 10.14
The Crash Site home page.

(continued from page 185)

His approach to Web-site design is a blend of technology and design sensibility. "This is sort of a golden age," he says. "Entry-level Web sites are pretty simple technically, but to do a really good job, you have to have an understanding of how it works. As sites get bigger and bigger, they become script-heavy and database-driven. If you're not technically savvy, you'll get left behind."

(continued on page 187) ▶

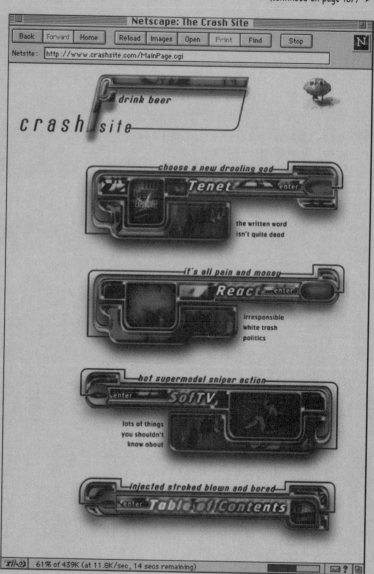

Figure 10.15
*Crash Site—
writing meets
design meets
the Web.*

(continued from page 186)

A good site balances technology with content—and poses both against the reader's reality, he says. He looks at his own work through a 14.4 modem at home . . . just to keep himself honest.

"You have to have something for everyone. The new technologies are almost a premium. You have to make it an entertaining experience for everyone. If they can get the new stuff, that's an added value.

"We concentrate on content before technology. We use real audio, GIF animation, cybercash for credit-card orders. But what people are raving about isn't technology; it's content—really good wiring and incredible graphics."

Being technology-savvy doesn't mean you need to be a programmer to build a good Web site—you just need to understand what technology means. "There are so many buzz words and buzz technologies flying around," he explains. "If you don't have an understanding of how these work, it is hard to tell if this is a good new thing or something that's been marketed well. You don't need to have the technical skills to administer a machine or write code, but you do need to understand the technology well enough to sort through it."

11
PUSHING THE ENVELOPE

Let's face it. There's only so much you can do with plain HTML. Eventually your site and your understanding of building Web pages reaches a point when you want to do more. Much more. You want to be able to push the envelope with your Web pages. It could be just some HTML tricks that extend your designs. It could be the addition of animation or sound into your pages. It could be new plug-in technology that extends your capabilities. It is most likely a combination of all the above. That's what this chapter is about: exploring next-step ways to extend your Web site in new ways.

plug-in technology—A way of expanding a browser's capability by adding (plugging in) new features.

But first, a word of warning. Some of the technical information in this chapter is likely to change from week to week. The Web progresses at an astounding rate, and it could be that some of this information is outdated even before this book makes it to print. The best place to find out about the latest technologies is online. One place to start is (you guessed it!) Project Cool, http://www.projectcool.com.

Also, if you are interested in a particular technology, stop by its vendor's Web site on a regular basis. For example, new versions of plug-in applications can appear as often as once a week—or as infrequently as once a quarter. Sometimes the changes are incremental, but sometimes they offer you new functionality or change the way you implement content in your site, so it's important to keep up with the latest.

ONE-PIXEL IMAGE TRICKS

Sometimes you want to adjust the placement of items on your screen by just a small amount. HTML isn't that precise, and what you could really use is some sort of spacer to force the alignment. Well, there's a fairly simple way to create that spacer. In fact, it's as simple as one dot.

What's the smallest size GIF image you can have? One pixel by one pixel, of course. Odds are that you've never considered having a picture that small. After all, what can you represent? The answer is: color. Remember the <img> tag? Remember the width and height attributes? Remember the fact that you can scale images with those switches? Imagine this: You need a one-color, 50-by-30-pixel block on the screen. You may not realize it, but you have an arsenal of single-color, single-pixel GIF images.

Figure 11.1 shows some of the things you can do with single-pixel GIFs. All of the boxes and rules are created from single-pixel GIFs. There are no large graphic files, and you have complete positioning control, one pixel at a time.

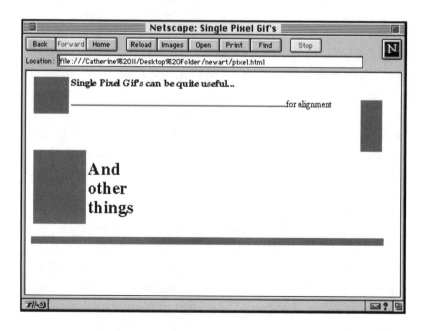

Figure 11.1
The variety of image and alignment tricks you can do with one-pixel GIFs.

Here is the code that created Figure 11.1. Notice that the one-pixel GIF is named "blue.gif." The same image is called in many places, but the width and height is different in each case, creating a rule, a bar, and a block. The align switch sends the shape to the right or left, and the text appears in the appropriate relationship to the GIF.

Imagine that the box in front of the words "And Other Things" was a transparent GIF rather than a blue one. You'd have created the effect of an indent of a specific size, even though HTML doesn't have an indent tag.

```
<html>
<head>
<title>Single Pixel Gif's</title>
</head>
<body bgcolor="ffffff">
<img src="images/blue.gif" width=50 height=50 align=left>
<h3>Single Pixel Gif's can be quite useful...</he>
<img src="images/blue.gif" width=30 height=70 align=right>
<img src="images/blue.gif" width=300 height=2>for alignment
<br clear=all>
<img src="images/blue.gif" width=75 height=100 align=left>
<h1>And<br>other<br>things</h1>
<br clear=all>
<img src="images/blue.gif" width=100% height=10>
</body>
```

One-pixel GIFs can be a very powerful layout tool if you think of them as one-unit building blocks rather than graphics.

To use a one-pixel graphic:

1. Go into Photoshop (or your graphics program of choice) and create a one-pixel-by-one-pixel indexed image in the color that you want to use.

2. Save the image. It will be a very tiny file.

3. Go to your HTML file. At the point in your HTML page where you want a block of color, a colorful rule,

or an index, insert your one-pixel GIF using the normal image tag.

```
<img src="red.gif"
```

4. Add the height and width switches to specify the size of the block.

```
<img src="red.gif" width=100 height=25
```

5. Add the align switch to specify the block's alignment.

```
<img src="red.gif" width=100 height=25 align=left
```

6. End the tag. That's all there is to using one-pixel GIFs.

```
<img src="red.gif" width=100 height=25 align=left>
```

 TRY THIS: Here are a few exercises that you might want to try for starters. In the Try It section, we have created three one-pixel GIF files that you can play with:

▶ A purple one-pixel image, purple.gif
▶ A green one-pixel image, green.gif
▶ A transparent one-pixel image, transparent.gif (for more about transparent GIFs, see the next section)

One-pixel GIFs can be stretched and shaped to create any rectangular color block you might need.

1. Make a 50 × 50 green box. Here is the tag you'd use:

```
<img src="green.gif" width=50 height=50>
```

2. Click on TRY IT to see the results.
3. You can stretch the GIF to fill any rectangular size you need. Edit that img tag to make it a 28 × 120 block of color and press TRY IT to see the results.

Tired of plain-looking horizontal rules? How about a purple one that fills 75 percent of the width of the browser window? Again, using a one-pixel image file, you can create a custom-color horizontal rule.

1. Make a 75 percent × 1 pixel purple rule. Here is the tag you'd use:

```
<img src="purple.gif" width=75% height=1>
```

2. Click on TRY IT to see the results.

3. Resize the browser window and watch how the rule stretches or shrinks to fill 75 percent of the new size.

4. Make the rule thicker. Edit the height to be three pixels and click on TRY IT to see the changes.

Need your paragraph indented 10 pixels? With HTML, there is no way to specify an indent. But put a transparent image in front of the paragraph, and you create the effect of an indent.

1. Type a paragraph tag and this line of text:

```
Once Upon A Time
<p>
In a Kingdom by the Sea
```

2. Click on TRY IT to see the result.

3. Now, insert a 10-pixel-wide, 250-pixel-deep green color block in front of the first line of text. Here is the tag you'd use:

```
<img src="green.gif" width=10 height=250
align=left>
Once Upon A Time
<p>
In a Kingdom by the Sea
```

4. Click on TRY IT to see the results.

5. Edit the img tag to use a transparent GIF instead of a green GIF. Here is the tag you'd use:

```
<img src="transparent.gif" width=10 height=1>
```

6. Click on TRY IT to see the results.

7. Try changing the width of the GIF to create different sizes of indents. To indent each line a different amount,

insert in front of each line of text a transparent GIF that is the width of indent you want by one pixel deep.

TRANSPARENT GIFs

A transparent GIF is an image in which one color has been selected to be transparent or invisible when the image is displayed on a Web page. This allows you to produce images that don't look rectangular and that show background colors and patterns through them. Photoshop allows you to export GIF images with a transparent color that you select. There are also many publicly available programs that allow you to set transparency in your GIF images; check the ftp archives for your particular computer system.

A word of advice when creating images with transparency: Always create the image on a background that is close in color to the background of your Web page. If not, you will see some pixels along the edges that clash with the rest of your display. This is called artifacting.

LOW SOURCE IMAGES

Another special effect you can add to your site is to have two images load into the same location. One image loads first, followed by the second. You create this through the lowsrc switch in the tag <img>. There are a couple of effects you can create with this technique. One is to load a black and white version of the image, followed by a color version of the same image. The black and white image loads quickly and gives your reader something to look at while the larger color image is downloading. The "colorization" look can also be used to nice effect with the right graphics.

Another item you can create with this effect is a slide show, in which one image follows another. Maybe your site is about the construction of a new building. You have an architect's sketch load first, followed by a simulated photo of how the new building will look. You've added a sense of

transparent GIF—A GIF file that appears transparent on your Web page.

artifacting—The pixel clash at the edge of a transparent GIF and the Web-page background.

lowsource (lowsrc)—A switch in <img> that lets you load one image atop another.

motion and time with basic HTML tags. To create this effect, include the lowsrc switch in <img>, like this:

```
<img lowsrc="images/face.gif" src="images/face2.gif" width=50
height=50>
```

When you use this tag, the browser will load the lowsrc image first. Then, once the entire Web page has loaded, the source image (src) will load on top of the lowsrc image. This allows you to have two totally different images in one place or to have minor variations of the same image.

Figures 11.2 and 11.3 show one way to use the low source/high source tag to create a simple two step animation. Figure 11.2 is the low source image; it loads first. Ideally, it should be a smaller file that loads quickly. After the entire page has loaded, Figure 11.3, which is the high source image, loads directly on top of Figure 11.2.

You can see the two-step process working in the Try It section. To see it, go to the Try It section and select the Lo/Hi option.

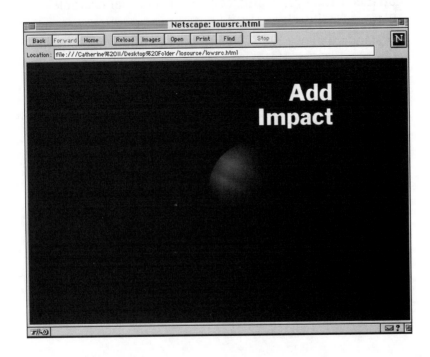

Figure 11.2
The first image that loads.

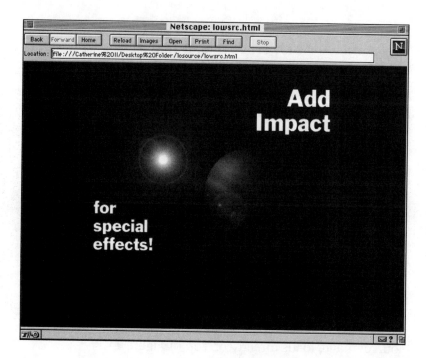

Figure 11.3
After the page has loaded, this image loads directly over the first image.

ANIMATED GIFS

As you've seen with transparent GIFs, GIF images hold more than meets the eye. Animated GIFs are another example of GIF functionality that can add interest to your Web site. The GIF standard allows you to place a series of images together into a single GIF and have the images play back as an animation when loaded on a Web page. Moving logos, animated buttons, cartoon characters, and special effects are all possible using GIF animations.

To create a GIF animation, all you need is a series of images that you've created and a software package that allows you to place them into a GIF animation. The software for creating these animations is just now starting to appear, so, as of this writing, we can't recommend any particular programs. You should be able to find a shareware program to do this from one of the ftp archives. The results, if not overused, are worth the effort it takes to create the images.

A few thoughts on using animated GIFs:

- ▶ Like other images, they fill bandwidth. Make sure the value of using them offsets any overhead they carry.

- ▶ Use animated GIFs in moderation. One might be just the right touch to grab the reader's eye—but a dozen blinking and flashing on one page is likely overkill.

- ▶ Try to keep the size of each image in the animated GIF to a reasonable size—remember, the full animation file's size is the cumulative total of all the individual images.

- ▶ Think about how the individual pieces work with each other. Remember, you are creating a moving image that your readers will see as one unit.

There are also some online resources that provide good information about GIF animations. We've collected them (and keep the URLs updated) at http://www.projectcool. com/guide/html/useful.html.

PLUG-IN POWER

You've probably heard about plug-ins. Plug-ins are programs that add new functionality to a Web browser by giving it capabilities that were not included in the browser itself. Plug-ins can handle graphics, sounds, animations, and more. Nearly anything anyone would want to do on the Web can be done via a plug-in. If it doesn't already exist, someone is likely figuring out how to program it right now, as you read these very words.

So, there are lot of plug-ins out there, and odds are you can find a plug-in to do what you want. You run out and buy the applications software to create content in that particular format. "Great!" you think. "I'm ready to enhance my site with it."

But wait, there's more to a plug-in that just creating content for it and incorporating it on your site. Your audience also has to have the plug-in player installed on their computers. After all, if they can't see what you've created, what good does it do to create it? With the number of plug-ins out there, no one has them all, which can leave one asking: Is it plug-in power . . . or plug-in confusion? The answer is, it's a little of both.

With plug-ins, you really have to focus on what goals you have for your site and who will be viewing it. One approach, if your audience is fairly broad, is to stick to the most common plug-ins and design for those. You can also put a link on your front page to the plug-in you use so that people might easily find the plug-in, install it, and come back. We do both of these for the Project Cool Web site. We use PDF (portable document format), which requires the Adobe Acrobat 3.0 plug-in. It's one of the common plug-ins, and we also link back to the site where users can get it if they don't have it.

The most common plug-ins are:

▶ PDF (Adobe Acrobat), which lets you put anything on the Web that you can create as a PostScript file. This includes real, antialiased fonts and complex graphical layouts.

▶ Shockwave, from Macromedia, which lets you add complex animations to your Web site.

▶ VRML, Virtual Reality Modeling Language, which is a way of creating and transmitting three-dimensional worlds that can be explored with one of the many VRML players.

Two other items you see on many Web sites are Real Audio and Java. Real Audio lets you include streaming audio in your site. Streaming audio is audio that begins to play as soon as it begins to download. To incorporate Real Audio, you must have a Real Audio server running. Using Real

streaming audio—Audio that begins to play as soon as it begins to download.

Audio is substantially more complex than working with a plug-in and is too detailed to teach in this chapter.

Java is a programming language that lets you add applets and special effects to a Web site. It, too, is far more complicated than the scope of this chapter, and your local bookstore shelves are likely filled with many guides to writing Java code.

PDF

Portable Document Format (PDF) is a format that allows you to view the same file in the same manner across different computer platforms. A PDF document looks the same whether it is viewed under UNIX, Mac, or Windows operating systems. It retains the format in which it was created and displays in clean, antialiased text on the user's monitor. With the Acrobat plug-in, a PDF file will display within a Web page or even within a browser window by itself.

> **PDF**—Portable Document Format, a file type viewed by the Acrobat plug-in.

The real beauty of PDF, though, is that you can use nearly anything to create content for it. Your desktop-publishing program, your spreadsheet program, your word-processing program . . . the rule of thumb is, if you can make a PostScript file, you can make a PDF file, which basically means that if you can print it, you can PDF it. Plus, you can add hyperlinks to the PDF document and firmly connect it to the Web or other PDF files. Another nice feature of PDF is that it is printable. If you are putting something on your Web site that you want people to be able to print in a certain format—say, a company brochure—PDF is an ideal technology.

To make the actual PDF file, you do need a PDF conversion program such as the Adobe Acrobat 3.0 package to create PDF, but the viewer your readers use is free and freely distributable. Once you have the Acrobat package, you can use anything that can print to create your PDF files.

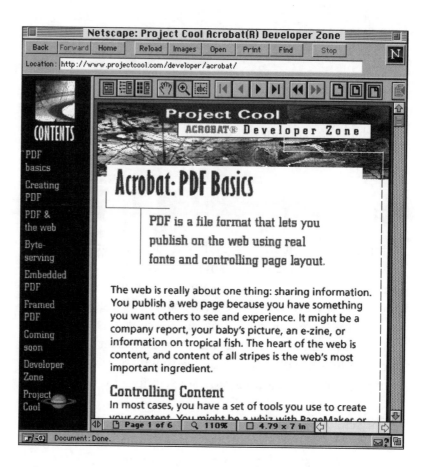

Figure 11.4
A PDF file embedded in an HTML page.

Figure 11.4 shows you what an example PDF file looks like on the Web. Notice the Acrobat buttons at the top of the page that allow you to zoom in and out, flip pages, and so on. These are all handy additional controls that make it easier to navigate through PDF documents. The HTML on the left side of the page is actually controlling which PDF files appear in the frame to the right.

Shockwave

Another major player in the plug-in arena is Macromedia's Shockwave. This is software that allows many multimedia capabilities to be pulled together into one file. The technology behind this is Macromedia's Director, which has been a standard for creating elaborate multimedia presentations and games.

Like PDF, it too requires that you own the creation software (Director), but the playback software is freely distributable. Whole books have been written on this technology, and if you are considering adding Shockwave to your Web site, a good resource to checkout is the *Lingo and Shockwave Sourcebook* (John Wiley & Sons), written by Vineel Shah and scheduled for publication in early 1997. It's an extremely powerful, though bandwidth-intensive, package, and as such has quite a learning curve in order to be able to exploit it fully.

Director is a professional-level multimedia program. If you plan on incorporating Shockwave into your Web site, you'll need to learn multimedia design skills or work with someone who already has them. If you use Shockwave, you'll want to use it well and take full advantage of its capabilities. If all you want is a simple animation, like a flashing sign, you might want to consider GIF animations instead. The Macromedia Web site has links to a number of Web sites the make good use of Shockwave. The best way to understand this technology is to experience it directly on your Web browser.

VRML

A third area of Web enhancements is VRML, Virtual Reality Modeling Language. VRML is a way of creating and transmitting three-dimensional worlds that can be explored, if, once again, your users have the appropriate plug-in installed. There are different VRML plug-ins for different browsers, but they all try to be compatible with the VRML standard. This technology perhaps holds the most intrigue, but it is often the most disappointing in that you need to have a high-end computer system with a high-speed net connection

> **Virtual Reality Modeling Language (VRML)—** A three-dimensional file type.

to fully enjoy it. In addition to PDF, Shockwave, and VRML, there are many, many other plug-ins and technologies available. Check sites like http://www.browserwatch.com for the most up-to-date information on new plug-ins.

These technologies, if targeted for your audience, can really add flash and dazzle to your Web sites, but don't be so blinded by what you can do that you forget about your end users. It's like everything else in Web design—a balance between possibility and reality, technology and design, your content and the reader's environment.

TABATHA HOLTZ, WEB DESIGNER, HUTCHINSON AVENUE SOFTWARE, MONTREAL/TORONTO, CANADA

TABATHA HOLTZ—WEB DEITY (www.tabatha.hasc.com)

Tabatha Holtz could be the poster girl for the way the Web can change a career. Holtz, 30, started out studying fine arts but found herself working as an administrative assistant. She was with the Ontario Teleprescense Project at the University of Toronto when the Project wanted to put its findings on the Web. Creating HTML pages was viewed by the computer scientists as something akin to grunt work, and the task landed on Tabatha.

"It was love at first sight. All I could say was 'wow,' " she says of the first time she saw the Web.

The Ontario Teleprescense Project was studying the sociological impacts of video conferencing. Everyone in the project, including Tabatha, had a speaker, microphone, camera, and computer on their desks. An application would take a photo every five minutes and send it to the server. The late Martin Friedmann, who was part of the project, wrote a script that turned the pictures of Tabatha into a QuickTime movie. The movies were hosted on Friedmann's Web site . . . and as Tabatha was coming to know the Web, the Web was coming to know Tabatha.

One thing led to another, and Tabatha's home page was born. It became a Cool Site of the Day (one of the Project Cool sites this book's coauthor, Glenn Davis, created), and Tabatha found job offers in her e-mail box. The transition from administrative assistant to Web deity was underway.

Today Tabatha designs Web pages for a living, and her original home page is still up and running. It remains one of the coolest personal pages on the Web.

"I use my home page to do a lot of experimenting," she says. I watch the feedback from readers, and the results help me in creating other pages."

(continued on page 204) ▶

(continued from page 203)

Figure 11.5
*Tabatha's home page
is always a work
in progress.*

That feedback and changeability is one of the greatest strengths of the Web, says Holtz. "It's dynamic and updatable in a second, unlike a CD-ROM, where the information doesn't change unless you go and buy another CD-ROM. On the Web, everything is fresh and new—if the person is updating it.

"When I change my home page, I can change the dynamics of it—not just the information. I can change what it *does,* not just what it contains. That's exciting."

Tabatha's Web philosophy focuses around simplicity. "You don't need a hundred and one toys on your page," she says.

"There's a difference between distraction and attention-grabbing. If it's annoying, it is a distraction. But if it stops me and makes me read it, then it is attention-grabbing."

(continued on page 205) ▶

(continued from page 204)

The trick, she says, lies in knowing the difference.

She also suggests avoiding text-heavy sites that overwhelm the reader. "Get to the point," she says. "Why am I (the reader) here? Why do I want to be here?"

But the real bottom line is simply doing the site well, whether it is a home page or a commercial site.

"Let's face it. We're all pretty shallow to a certain extent." she says. "If something looks beautiful we're all apt to stick around and enjoy it, whereas if something is badly done, we're less likely to stay around."

Figure 11.6
Cats in Canada Web site where visitors can shop for or sell a cat or kitten.

12

THE ELUSIVE COOL SITE

As you've been reading this book, you've been seeing ideas for building Web sites and learning some design tips and guidelines. But we haven't talked about the nature of *cool*. We often get asked what *cool* is—and how to make a cool Web site. It seems that the elusive cool site is something that everyone wants—but no one is quite sure exactly what it is.

We've given the topic a lot of thought and consideration, and our answer is: We can't define it, either! Or, more precisely, only you can know for yourself.

You see, *cool* is a little like life. Someone else can hand out general guidelines, but there are no hard and fast rules— no matter how hard you look, there just isn't a single handbook to *cool*. In fact, sometimes breaking all the rules is what creates *cool*. In large part, building a cool site is about understanding the ebb and flow of the medium, what it can do, and how it is experienced. Guides get you started; the rest is up to you.

Learning to make Web sites has some parallels to learning to cook. At first you follow instructions that say: one tablespoon minced garlic, ¼ cup olive oil, and half an onion finely chopped. Then, you start to really understand the elements. You know the smell of garlic and how it mingles with the oil. You experience and begin to understand on a deeper level how fine mincing and coarse mincing changes the way the oil absorbs the garlic flavor. You start to sense how onion fits into the mix. And then you start to vary the recipe to create the dish that matches your—and your audience's—taste more exactly: a little more garlic, a little less onion, extra virgin oil, maybe a hint of white pepper. . . .

This book shows you how to make HTML code and gives some basic guidelines for building good sites. But to make really cool sites, you need to absorb the medium and begin to feel how a little more animation balances with a little less text for your site. This takes time. It takes practice. And it takes hands-on immersion in the medium. By hands-on immersion, we don't just mean that you keep practicing building Web sites, but that you look at the good sites that are out there and learn by their example. After all, if you want to be a great director, you watch great movies. If you want to be a great writer, you read the great novels. If you want to build cool Web sites . . . well, you get the idea.

The magic of a cool site is difficult to define. Much of it is that sense that the whole is greater than the sum of its parts. It's the way the content suddenly seems "made for the Web." It's that indefinable *it* that lifts one site above the ordinary.

What we do know, though, are some ways to frame the idea of *cool* that might help you find your answer to the question of what it is. Here's a half dozen lenses that we look through when we're thinking about a site and testing its cool factor.

COOL RULE #1: IT'S ALL IN THE EYE OF THE BEHOLDER

The first thing to remember is that there is no single definition of *cool*. *Cool* is a lot of different things. What you, your six-year-old daughter, and your grandfather think is *cool* is likely to be different. *Cool* on the Web is framed by your real-life experiences and expectations.

That line of thought sends us back to one of the most important elements in Web site design: your audience. Yes, we've said it before, but it can't be overstated enough: Web sites don't exist in a vacuum. There's you, the creator. There are your readers. And there are the wires and computers in between. All three factors combine to create the Web experience. And the Web really is an experience. It draws on multiple senses. It is an active event. It's participatory. It requires interaction.

Understand what look and feel appeals to your readers, what graphics hit their hot buttons, what content calls out to their ears and eyes. It doesn't matter if you're creating a personal page or a corporate page—if you're out of touch with your readers, nothing you do will feel cool to them.

There's a preteen "Lifestyle Magazine" section in the Tampax brand site that doesn't do much for us, but the 13-year-old girls who use it seem to love it. They are the people for whom the section is designed. They are the audience, and it is cool to them. And that's what matters.

COOL RULE #2: BE TRUE TO YOURSELF

Knowing what appeals to your audience, that's the first step. But remember, you are part of the equation too. You have a look and a feel all your own, and you come with a set of expectations. Be yourself!

Cool is largely a matter of perception. It can't be forced. If you try to force it, you end up with the "tragically hip" syndrome. You end up looking like someone's fortysomething mom in a mosh pit awkwardly trying to be . . . well . . . cool.

We remember seeing one Web site for a company that built boards for PCs. The company's overall image was pretty subdued and serious . . . but its Web site was from a different planet. One can almost hear somebody saying, "Hey, you gotta be cool in your Web site." This company's pages used an odd array of very bright colors and an excessive variety of type. It was as if the designer wanted to make it like *Wired* but saw only the unconventional use of type and color and missed the underlying structure and brand-consistent look and feel of the magazine. This PC board company's resulting Web site was most definitely not cool.

Being cool is presenting yourself in the right light, not tossing away your audience's expectations of your brand image. *Cool* rings true at its core—and to be cool, your site needs to ring true, too.

COOL RULE #3: COOL ISN'T STATIC

That which is defined as *cool* can change from day to day. *Cool* can never rest on its laurels; it must always keep up with the ever changing world and Web.

Remember, perception is shaped by the experiences of the individual. If your site is the first place your readers have ever seen an animated GIF, that blinking green light is going to look pretty cool. But by the time they've visited 16 sites, each using an animated GIF better than the one before it, yours will just wilt in comparison. Even worse if their animated GIF is the same one as yours.

Go out and rent the original *Star Wars* for a great example of experience shifting perception. When *Star Wars* first came out, we were awed by the special effects. We'd never seen anything like it, and the impression was just incredible. Some of us saw it seven or eight times. Today, it's still a good movie, but its effects look pretty basic.

All of which isn't to say that flash, dazzle, and the latest technology will make your site cool. Alone, they won't. But a site can't languish, either. The stakes are constantly shifting, and you need to be aware of the changes around you—not only in technology, but in reader expectation.

COOL RULE #4: DON'T BE RANDOM

There's a point to having a Web site—or at least there should be. You have a goal you want to accomplish with it. Maybe that goal is as simple as telling the world you're online. Or maybe it involves relaying a marketing message. Or perhaps it's about presenting information on a specific topic and building readership to sell advertising. Whatever the goal, it is important to know it, to embrace it, and to let it be obvious.

Cool isn't random cool stuff. *Cool* does have a purpose but doesn't need to flaunt it. You can create a site that sells fine silk blouses and do it in a very elegant, effective manner. Or, you create a crass, shove-the-goods-down-their-throat site. The end is the same—to sell merchandise. But one site stands out and above as an example of Web-done-well; the other is so full of itself that it just reinforces every bad image anyone ever had about online commerce.

There are sites out there that think they are cool, but in reality they are nothing but ego stops. They have no purpose but to pose and posture. Strip away the pretentious graphics or the flashy implementation of Java and there is nothing underneath. Substance makes a site sing.

There are some excellent text sites. The Bartleby Library project at Columbia University isn't doing anything flashy . . . but it *is* cool, because it is putting high-quality content online in a clean, clear, accessible way. It doesn't need to strut—its purpose and substance make it stand out.

COOL RULE #5: QUALITY, QUALITY, QUALITY

The quality of each element of the site combines to create an end result—if you've got typos and sloppy graphics, you get a site that exists. Period. But, if you have scintillating text, artful graphics, and a well-planned technical execution, you're well on your way to *cool*.

Writing

It is amazing how many sites out there seem to have forgotten Mrs. Baker's third-grade grammar rules. Or have never heard of the concept of proofreading. Or simply decided writing wasn't important enough to qualify for effort, attention, or professionalism.

No one is perfect, and the occasional slip-up is inevitable. We wish our site were typo-free, but from time to time, one reader or another e-mails us to point out an error, a typo, a misspelling, or a duplicate word. We fix them, we proof some more, and we acknowledge that we can never proof enough. And we cringe every time. Don't get so pulled into the speed of creating and posting that you forget the basics, that you forget to take time to read what you've written and to see it with an editor's keen eye.

The quality of writing is important. We were reading an essay in CrashSite and forgot we were using the Web . . . the interface just faded away and the words took over, propelling us forward. The same happened with a lyrical description of a neon-fronted motel in the Motel Americana site. Great writing overrides virtually everything.

Graphics

The quickest way to make your site look like a *Gong Show* entrant is to use poorly done graphics. Want to look like rank amateur? Just use that rainbow-colored rule six or eight times on your page. Want to look like someone who just discovered computers? Then be sure to include some hyper-over-Kai-Power Tools-altered buttons.

Graphics are part of your site's overall look and feel. Keep them appropriate to the mood and tone, and keep them quality.

That doesn't mean your graphics have to be slick. If the feel of your site is homey, then use simple, comfy graphics. There are a range of styles, each equally good. The only styles you should avoid are sloppy, trite, and overused.

If you're a commercial site, spring for an artist or illustrator. As we learned in desktop publishing, simply having a tool doesn't turn someone into a jack-of-all-trades overnight. It's not fair to either your staff or your Web site to ask your copy editors to draw complex illustrations of your product line to put on the Web just because you put Illustrator or Freehand on their Macs.

Design

We've talked a lot about design in this book. The only note to add here is to execute it well. Be organized, be clean, and show that you care about your design. Once again, quality counts.

Content

A cool site has content worth coming to visit. Content should be accurate. It should be clear. It should be accessible.

The content pieces need to work together. Do the photos match the text? Do the search results have meaning? Does the design show the reader what to do next?

There are some sites that are nothing but sets of links. When the links are tied together with a theme and some introductory text, they might comprise good content. For example, there is a site that is nothing but television-industry links. It is very useful. But there are a number of sites that are nothing but random lists of links presented in one long list. Is this compelling content?

The *what* of the content not only needs to be compelling, but it also needs to be well done. If it's news, that means fresh and truthful. If it's a game, that means excellent graphics and good play. If it's a novel, that means excellent writing. If it's an art site, that means interesting art, presented well. This sounds obvious, right? But spend 15 minutes surfing the Web and you'll see that, for many people who build Web pages, it isn't.

Technical Execution

The Web relies on a variety of technologies to deliver an information experience to your readers. We hesitate to call it a viewing experience, because readers do more than sit back and watch. And it isn't a reading experience because they do more than read. It can be a multifaceted experience that engages them on many levels . . . if you implement the right technology well.

There are multiple ways to produce any given page. The method you select will have a direct effect on the way your site is perceived. You need to understand the pros and cons of the different technologies. But that's not all. You need to execute the one you select with the utmost skill.

Part of *cool* is understanding the tools and using the best for each job.

Use of the Medium

What does your site do that you can't do with paper or video? If the answer is "nothing," then you probably aren't using the Web well.

One of the cool things about the Web in general is all the things it lets you do that you can't do in any other medium. Hyperlink. Search. Interact. Let people talk to you. Let people follow their own path. Use audio and text at the same time, supporting each other. This sounds a little academic, but with the Web, we really are able to create a different paradigm for communication, learning, and information dissemination.

No one has completely figured out all that the Web can do, and as new technologies appear and bandwidth limitations disappear, the way we use the Web is likely to change again and again. Part of *cool* is making use of every advantage you have, gracefully and with style.

COOL RULE #6:
THE SUM OF THE PARTS . . .

The Web is a web of pieces, all woven together. Your site is, too. Each piece needs to be good-quality and able to stand on its own. But to be cool, the whole must be greater than the sum of its parts.

A leather jacket doesn't make you cool. Nor does a silk scarf, a black T-shirt, or any other accessory alone. It is the total look that says *cool.*

The same is true for your Web site. Synergy is important. It's the element that generates that hard-to-define "wow" response. It's like the horse taking the jump at exactly the right millisecond, with every muscle moving together, and the rider at just the right angle in the saddle, creating a feeling that horse and rider are one, centaurlike creature. It's like finding the "slot" on a sailboat, where the boat surges forward and seems to sail itself and come to life.

A cool site is one where the magic works.

Cool is often a gut instinct. That instinct is usually right for a reason, a reason that you can usually uncover if you sit back and analyze it. Listen to your gut—it knows things your mind doesn't admit to.

You know, it's like cooking again. Intellectually, you can sort out the right proportions of sugar to cinnamon, but your nose and tongue really know best. They can sense what your mind is hard-pressed to figure out.

If something feels right for your site, go with it. Try it. Test it and see what kind of reaction it gets. Nothing is permanent in cyberspace, and you can always change it if you don't like it. Watch what you do, what choices you make, and learn. Learn the pulse of the medium. Learn the flow of the technology. Learn what works for you.

One of the authors was being interviewed by a reporter one time, and the reporter asked him: "Is your cool James Dean cool or *Beavis and Butthead* cool?" Glenn thought for a few moments and responded: "Neither. It's Glenn Davis cool."

When it comes to *cool,* the only way to find that elusive beast is to look within yourself. We all have it inside us, and it takes different forms for different people, just as it takes different forms for different Web sites. So, when you're pondering the meaning of *cool,* just remember this—the *cool* you want is *your* cool. Because that's what *cool* is really all about.

APPENDIX A
HTML TAG QUICK REFERENCE

BASIC HTML TAGS

These tables summarize the basic HTML tags.

Document structure

Function	Tag	Switches	Ending tag
HTML file	\<html>	none	\</html>
File header	\<head>	none	\</head>
File title	\<title>	none	\</title>
File comments	\<!>	text of comment	none
File body	\<body>	background="*filename*"	\</body>
		bgcolor="*xxxx*"	
		text="*xxxx*"	
		link="*xxxx*"	
		vlink="*xxxx*"	

Basic text

Function	Tag	Switches	Ending tag
Line break	\ 	clear=left/right	none
Paragraph	\<p>	align=center/right	none
Bold	\<b>	none	\</b>
Italic	\<i>	none	\</i>
Typewriter text	\<tt>	none	\</tt>
Headline	\<h1–6>	align=center/right	\</h1–6>
Font	\<font>	size=+/–*xxx*	\</font>
Horizontal rule	\<hr>	size=*xx*	none
		width=*xx*/*xx*%	
		noshade	
Block quote	\<blockquote>	none	\</blockquote>

Lists

Function	Tag	Switches	Ending tag
Unordered list	<ul>	type=disc/circle/square	</ul>
Ordered list	<ol>	type=I/A/1/a/i	</ol>
		start=*xx*	
List item	<li>	type=disc/circle	
		/square/I/A/1/a/i	none
Definition list	<dl>	none	</dl>
Definition-list item	<dt>	none	none
Definition-list definition	<dd>	none	none

Linking tags

Function	Tag	Switches	Ending tag
Anchor	<a>	href="*filename*"	</a>
Anchor mark	<a>	name="*markname*"	none

Image tags

Function	Tag	Switches	Ending tag
Insert image	<img>	src="*filename*"	none
		align=left/right	
		width=*xxx*	
		height=*xxx*	
		alt="*text*"	
		ismap	
		usemap="*#mapname*"	
		lowscr="*filename*"	

Client-side map tags

Function	Tag	Switches	Ending tag
Define map	<map>	name="*mapname*"	</map>
Area definition	<area>	shape="rect/circle/poly/point"	none
		coords="*x,y,x,y*"	
		href="*imagename*"	

Table tags

Function	Tag	Switches	Ending tag
Table	<table>	border=x width=x cellspacing=x cellpadding=x bgcolor="xxxx"	</table>
Table row	<tr>	align=left/center/right valign=top/middle/bottom bgcolor="xxxx"	</tr>
Table data	<td>	align=left/center/right valign=top/middle/bottom width=x nowrap colspan=x rowspan=x bgcolor="xxxx"	</td>
Table header	<th>	align=left/center/right valign=top/middle/bottom width=x nowrap colspan=x rowspan=x bgcolor="xxxx"	</th>
Caption	<caption>	align=left/center/right valign=top/middle/bottom	</caption>

Frames tags

Function	Tag	Switches	Ending tag
Start frame set	<frameset>	cols="xx/xx%/*" rows="xx/xx%/*"	</frameset>
Frame	<frame>	scr="filename" name="framename" noresize scroll=auto/yes/no	none
Base	<base>	target="framename"	none
No frames	<noframes>	none	</noframes>

Form tags

Function	Tag	Switches	Ending tag
Form	\<form>	method=get/post action="*program name*"	\</form>
Input field	\<input>	name="*variable name*" type=text/password/ checkbox/radio/ submit/reset/image	none
Selection list	\<select>	name="*variable name*" size=*xx* multiple	\</select>
Selection option	\<option>	none	none
Scrolling text field	\<textarea>	name="*variable name*" rows=*xx* cols=*xx*	\</textarea>

Common special characters

Name	Character	Code sequence
ampersand	&	&
cent sign	¢	¢
degree sign	°	°
greater than	>	>
less than	<	<
nonbreaking space		

APPENDIX B
COLOR NAMES AND HEX VALUES

This table summarizes the common standardized color names and their hexadecimal values.

Color	Hex value	Color	Hex value
aliceblue	f0f8ff	darkgreen	006400
antiquewhite	faebd7	darkkhaki	bdb76b
aqua	00ffff	darkmagenta	8b008b
aquamarine	7fffd4	darkolivegreen	556b2f
azure	f0ffff	darkorange	ff8c00
beige	f5f5dc	darkorchid	9932cc
bisque	ffe4c4	darkred	8b0000
black	000000	darksalmon	e9967a
blanchedalmond	ffebcd	darkseagreen	8fbc8f
blue	0000ff	darkslateblue	483d8b
blueviolet	8a2be2	darkslategray	2f4f4f
brown	a52a2a	darkturquoise	00ced1
burlywood	deb887	darkviolet	9400d3
cadetblue	5f9ea0	deeppink	ff1493
chartreuse	7fff00	deepskyblue	00bfff
chocolate	d2691e	dimgray	696969
coral	ff7f50	dodgerblue	1e90ff
cornflowerblue	6495ed	firebrick	b22222
cornsilk	fff8dc	floralwhite	fffaf0
crimson	dc143c	forestgreen	228b22
cyan	00ffff	fuchsia	ff00ff
darkblue	00008b	gainsboro	dcdcdc
darkcyan	008b8b	ghostwhite	f8f8ff
darkgoldenrod	b8b60b	gold	ffd700
darkgray	a9a9a9	goldenrod	daa520

Color	Hex value	Color	Hex value
gray	808080	navy	000080
green	008000	oldlace	fdf5e6
greenyellow	adff2f	olive	808000
honeydew	f0fff0	olivedrab	6b8e23
hotpink	ff69b4	orange	ffa500
indianred	cd5c5c	orangered	ff4500
indigo	4b0082	orchid	da70d6
ivory	fffff0	palegoldenrod	eee8aa
khaki	f0e68c	palegreen	98fb98
lavender	e6e6fa	paleturquoise	afeeee
lavenderblush	fff0f5	palevioletred	db7093
lawngreen	7cfc00	papayawhip	ffefd5
lemonchiffon	fffacd	peachpuff	ffdab9
lightblue	add8e6	peru	cd853f
lightcoral	f08080	pink	ffc0cd
lightcyan	e0ffff	plum	dda0dd
lightgoldenrodyellow	fafad2	powderblue	b0e0e6
lightgreen	90ee90	purple	800080
lightgrey	d3d3d3	red	ff0000
lightpink	ffb6c1	rosybrown	bc8f8f
lightsalmon	ffa07a	royalblue	4169e1
lightseagreen	20b2aa	saddlebrown	8b4513
lightskyblue	87cefa	salmon	fa8072
lightslategray	778899	sandybrown	f4a460
lightsteelblue	b0c4de	seagreen	2e8b57
lightyellow	ffffe0	seashell	fff5ee
lime	00ff00	sienna	a0522d
limegreen	32cd32	silver	c0c0c0
linen	faf0e6	skyblue	87ceed
magenta	ff00ff	slateblue	6a5acd
maroon	800000	slategray	708090
mediumaquamarine	66cdaa	snow	fffafa
mediumblue	0000cd	springgreen	00ff7f
mediumorchid	ba55d3	steelblue	4682b4
mediumpurple	9370db	tan	d2b48c
mediumseagreen	3cb371	teal	008080
mediumslateblue	7b68ee	thistle	d8bfd8
mediumspringgreen	00fa9a	tomato	ff6347
mediumturquoise	48d1cc	turquoise	40e0d0
mediumvioletred	c71585	violet	ee82ee
midnightblue	191970	wheat	f5deb3
mintcream	f5fffa	white	ffffff
mistyrose	ffe4e1	whitesmoke	f5f5f5
moccasin	ffe4b5	yellow	ffff00
navajowhite	ffdead	yellowgreen	a9cd32

APPENDIX C

STANDARDS? WHAT STANDARDS?

Netscape Navigator, Internet Explorer, Mosaic . . . whose HTML is the correct HTML? The shocking truth? All of them. Which makes the Web builders' work that much more challenging.

A LITTLE HISTORY

In the beginning there was W3C, The World Wide Web Consortium (http://www.w3.org). It had a standards committee that decided what features should be included in HTML. This was fine and good, but standards committees operate at the speed of, well, committees. As the standards folks debated, the Web sped on, evolving at a rapid clip.

Meanwhile, companies like Netscape added HTML features that browser users and early Web builders were asking for, such as left and right image alignment. The Web had such momentum that it was moving forward regardless of what the overseeing standards body did.

In an interesting flip, the committee tacitly acknowledged this by agreeing to consider the existing new features. Now, whenever something becomes widely used in HTML, the committee looks at it and decides whether to include it in the current standard. Often, the feature becomes a standard . . . and then the other browser manufacturers scramble to include it in their latest release of their latest browser.

So the term *standard* is a little fuzzy. It is more of a *de facto* set of standards, or one that is formalized after the fact. Industry observers say that's the way it should be with technology standards, that the market moves too fast to wait for committees to make decisions, that the developers and vendors have a better sense of the pulse of the market.

That is partly true. But as Web builders it is important to keep one eye open so that we don't find ourselves building three different versions of the same product for the different flavors of HTML. You can see where that splintered approach got the operating system UNIX: There are so many flavors of UNIX (AIX, IRIX, Solaris, etc.) that often the UNIX software you want doesn't run on your hardware's particular UNIX variety. And about every two years there's a chorus of "UNIX is dying," partly because the UNIX market feels like it is always feuding with itself.

What does this do to HTML? Well, it certainly jumbles the situation. Currently there is a core set of HTML tags that everyone seems to agree on. These are the tags that this book covers. There are also tags that just one browser or another uses but that not everyone supports. This appendix touches on a few of these. But remember—if you choose to use these tags, not all of you readers may be able to see the results. And, if you choose to use these tags, make sure they don't destroy the site for readers with another browser.

BROWSER WARS

Not only is HTML threatening to splinter, but the browsers themselves are evolving at a rapid clip, too. We're currently running Navigator 3.0 and Microsoft's Internet Explorer 3.0—this week, at least.

We've watched Navigator go from version .9 to the now current 3.0 in a matter of two years. By the time you read this you may be using Galileo (codename for Navigator 4.0). Meanwhile, Microsoft has just released—with much fanfare—IE 3.0 for the PC, with a Macintosh version promised before the end of 1996. Just weeks after the August 1996 release it announced IE 4.0.

At the time of this writing the competition is really focused on two browsers. As you might have guessed, they are Netscape's Navigator 3.0 and Microsoft's Internet Explorer 3.0. Each browser offers certain functionality and supports certain HTML tags that the other doesn't.

The functionality and user interface options are a matter of personal preference. Some people like one shape of button while others like another. Or maybe you are on a hardware platform that supports only one or the other. There are all good competitive differences.

The place where the red flag goes up for Web builders is in the HTML tags each browser supports. If you want to use a particular feature that may not yet be a blessed standard, it is important to know whether all browsers support it. And if they don't, you will need to find out if most of your audience will be able to see the effect you want to create.

Javascript is a good example of this. Javascript is a scripting language that lets you add certain types of actions to your site. Those scrolling text lines you see in the message bar of a browser are one of the most common Javascript applications. Both Netscape and Microsoft say they support Javascript, but despite what the companies say, the definition of *support* seems to vary. We recently wanted to implement a modest little effect using Javascript that turned a screen icon on and off. In this case, it turned out that IE didn't support this particular script, although the effect worked beautifully under Navigator.

So even Javascript can't be considered standard. And to further confuse matters for Web scripting standards, Microsoft has incorporated VBScript in Internet Explorer. The "VB" in VBScript stands for—surprise, surprise—Visual Basic, the Microsoft language that VBScript is based upon. With Microsoft and Netscape being such rivals right now, we can't imagine Netscape incorporating VBScript into Navigator. We are hoping, though, that Microsoft will more fully implement Javascript in the next version of their browser.

Neither of the browsers is always the leader. IE 3.0 is first out the door in support style sheets, a feature set that the W3C has endorsed. Navigator 3.0 does not support style sheets, although Netscape has said publicly that it will in its 4.0 release.

We find it rather odd, however, that Netscape is waiting this long to support style sheets; style sheets have been part of the standards proposal for over a year now, and both Netscape and Microsoft are members of the standards body.

Frames is another example where the two companies played catch-up with each other.

Netscape created frames first.

Then IE supported frames.

And then IE supported a feature that allowed for border-less frames.

Now Netscape supports that also—and lets you change the color of the frame border.

Microsoft has upped the ante, and under IE you can have a frame that is floating on the page in place of an image.

We suspect that this feature war will go on. And it is a healthy thing. By baiting each other back and forth, these companies are creating a richer environment for people to build and browse the Web, even if it makes it a little bumpy for the early adopters.

We don't have the space to show you these evolving HTML techniques, and since they are not all standard, they could change by the time you read this. We will, however, overview some of the highlights and show you where to go on the Web to learn more.

NAVIGATOR EXTRAS

Netscape Navigator supports a number of nice HTML features. The best place for the latest information about Netscape features is through the Navigator browser. The HELP button connects you with Netscape's latest release notes.

Multicolumn Text

This feature uses the tag <multicol>. Multicolumns let you specify the number of text columns within a browser window. When the browser sees the tag, the page is divided into the specified number of columns, and the text is flowed into it.

There are three switches:

► *cols=XX*

► *width=XX*

► *gutter=XX*

The value you enter for *cols* is the number of columns. For example, to produce a five-column layout within the browser window, you'd enter this tag:

```
<multicol cols=5>
```

The value you enter for the width switch is the width of each column.

The value you enter for the gutter switch is the space, in pixels, between each column.

If you omit either the width or space switch, the browser will calculate the value for you.

Be careful, though. This is a tag that could be abused very easily. Picture documents that are 9 screens tall with two columns—when you get to the bottom of one column, you then need to scrooooooll back to the top to keep reading. If you do use this tag, use it wisely. Keep your columns short so that people don't have to work to read your pages. Netscape provides control for the number of columns, their width, and the space between them, but no one can control the size of the user's browser window.

Spacing

This feature uses the tag <spacer>. Spacing lets you insert horizontal, vertical, and block spacing. This function is like a single-pixel GIF trick with its own tag.

There are five switches.

- ▶ *type= horizontal/vertical/block*
- ▶ *size= number of pixels*
- ▶ *width= number of pixels*
- ▶ *height= number of pixels*
- ▶ *align= left or right*

The type switch has three possible values: horizontal, vertical, and block. The value you enter here interacts with the pixel sizes and alignment you enter in the other switches.

- ▶ A horizontal spacer inserts horizontal space between words. The width of the space is controlled by the value you place in the size switch.

- A vertical spacer inserts vertical space between lines. This is a bit like going back to the days of handset type, where an extra bar of leading was inserted after each line of type to add extra space. Like the horizontal spacer, the size of the vertical spacer is defined by the value you place in the size switch.

- A block spacer is like a transparent GIF. You define the size of the block by using the width, height, and align switches. Set the values in the width, height, and align switches just as you do in the image tag (<img>).

TIP: *Until this feature is adopted by the W3C and is included in IE, we recommend that you stick with single-pixel GIFs, which will work across all browsers.*

Strikeout and Underline

There are two additional text-formatting tags.

The tag <strikeout> creates text with a strikeout bar though it. You'll need to end the text with the </strikeout> tag.

The tag <underline> creates underlined text. You'll need to end the text with the </underline> tag.

Think carefully about when you would treat text this way. Typically, strikeout is used as part of revision control. In typewritten copy, underline is used for emphasis or for book titles, but when text is typeset, one typically uses italic for these notations. On the Web, underline is often used to indicated links; in fact, this is the browser default, and by using underlined text elsewhere you could confuse some of your readers.

Font

The tag <font> now has an additional switch, *face.* The face= switch lets you specify a font by name. The browser looks on the user's local computer for the font.

You can call any font by any name. For example, if you want readers to see a font named Dancer, you'd enter the font tag like this:

```
<font face="Dancer">
```

You can also specify a string of faces that the browser will look for until it finds one that matches. For example, if Dancer is your first choice, Prancer your second, and Times your third, you'd enter the font tag like this:

```
<font face="Dancer,Prancer,Times">
```

TIP: *This feature is also supported in IE. However, IE also supports a set of style tags that are part of the much-larger style sheet standard outlined in the Microsoft section.*

For more details on Navigator enhancements, you should make a habit of checking the release notes for the version of Navigator that you are using. You can get to the release notes directly from your Navigator browser by clicking on HELP. The current Navigator 3.0 release notes can be found at this URL:

```
http://home.netscape.com/eng/mozilla/3.0/relnotes
```

INTERNET EXPLORER EXTRAS

Internet Explorer also supports a number of nice HTML features. The best place for the latest information about IE features is on the Microsoft Sitebuilder Workshop at

```
http://www.microsoft.com/workshop
```

Sound Files

Although this was initially a feature of IE 2.0, it is worth mentioning here because it is a nice added-value item to incorporate if most of your readers are using IE. With IE, you can have a short piece of music as background to each page.

For example, if you go to our home page at www.project-cool.com, you'll hear a movement from Moonlight Sonata. This is a MIDI file that is called in our HTML. Navigator readers don't hear it, but the lack of it doesn't interfere with using the site, either.

The sound option is supported through an HTML tag called background sound, <bgsound>. This tag has two switches:

- ▶ *src= name of sound file*
- ▶ *loop= number of times to repeat that file*

For example, to play a sound file named moonlight just once (no repeats), the tag would look like this:

```
<bg src="/sounds/"moonlight" loop=0>
```

Floating Frames

The floating frames feature is a new addition with IE 3.0. It allows you to have a frame positioned anywhere in the Web browser.

You create this effect with a new tag, <iframe>.

This feature opens up a new world of ideas for Web pages. For a full exploration of floating frames, visit either the Project Cool Developer Zone or Microsoft's support pages.

Tables

The table tag has received numerous enhancements in IE 3.0. You can now specify not only background colors for individual table cells but also background images. That means your individual table can have an image behind it, much as a page can.

You do this through the background switch. For example, to put in a background image named "fish.gif," your code might look like this:

```
<table background="/images/"fish.gif">
```

You can now create complex cells with text and graphics overlaying each other.

You can also specify what borders and rules to show and not to show for different table effects. You do this by adding the rules switch to the table or table row tag.

The rules switch has three values: rows, cols, or none.

▶ To turn on the horizontal rules between rows, use the switch like this:

```
<table rules =rows>
```

▶ To turn on the vertical rules between columns, use the switch like this:

```
<table rules =cols>
```

▶ To put a border around the outside of the table only, use the switch like this:

```
<table rules =none>
```

Font

IE supports the same additional font tag switch, *face=*, that Navigator does. Full support of other font attributes are controlled by the style tag, described next in this appendix.

Style

The style tag brings exciting additions to the Web builder's tool box.

TIP: *But remember, as of this writing, only IE 3.0 supports these tags, so if your readers are primarily Netscape users, they won't be able to see the results of these tags.*

Even if you are dealing with a Netscape world, you should still get your hands on a copy of IE and play with style sheets. Netscape says that its next version of Navigator will support style sheets, and you'll be a step ahead of the pack if you understand how they work.

The style tag lets you define most of the display characteristics that can apply to text. These include face, size, leading, indent, and a host of others. These are the type of controls that really add to information presentation on the Web.

But it gets better. You don't need to enter and reenter this tag and its chain of values. With cascading style sheets, you can build an index that describes how to display the different HTML attributes on a page. For example, you can set an <H1> tag so that it displays as Goudy Bold, 36 point, centered.

This is slightly like the idea behind SGML, a markup language used by government, defense, and other creators of huge documents that need to be viewed in different environments. The tags define the document parts, while a separate style guide defines how to display those body parts. The display elements, such as font style or margin indent, reside separately from the content.

This means changing the look and feel of a document is quite easy. You simply make a change in the style sheet and every document that references that style sheet changes. So if you decide you don't like that 36 point headline, you can tell the style sheet to display <H1> tags in 24 point Futura Light. With no more effort than that, all the HTML files that reference the style sheet now display <H1> headlines in the new format.

Style sheets are quite powerful. We recommend you go to Microsoft's Workshop (http://www.microsoft.com/workshop) for the latest information on what aspects of style sheets IE is supporting.

PREPARING FOR THE FUTURE

You can't be too sure of the future of Web development. New ideas and tools seem to be popping up daily. Keep your eyes open, and watch HTML and other technologies evolve.

From HTML editing tools to animated GIF building blocks to color-matching systems for the Web, the suite of possible tools grows longer every day. Don't let yourself be overwhelmed by it—if you find a tool that works for you, use it. But if something interesting comes by, don't be afraid to give it a try, either.

Pay close attention to Java, Javascript, and ActiveX, as they appear to hold the keys to our possible futures. These programming and scripting languages intersect the worlds of the design and programming communities; they are the types of tools that let us add new levels of action and interactivity to the Web.

There is a lifetime of learning out there on the Web. In fact, as we create our respective pages and sites, we are actually building our own future at the same time.

No one can learn it all at once. Instead, focus on what works best across the different platforms and for your audience, and you'll be creating great Web sites.

And one final note—don't forget to throw in a bit of attitude for good measure. Complacency makes the Web a dull place—and one that has stopped evolving. Let that nosy child who lives inside your head come out to play sometimes, and the Web will be a more interesting, fluid, and rewarding place.

INDEX

INDEX